D1128801

EDITED BY JULIE
& SIMON FREEMAN

RUNNING WILD

INSPIRATIONAL TRAILS FROM AROUND THE WORLD

WITH OVER 200 ILLUSTRATIONS

FOREWORD BY DEAN KARNAZES

LIKE THE WIND

CONTENTS

FOREWORD

by Dean Karnazes

Inside each of us is a wild animal yearning to escape. Being outdoors in nature is fundamental to who we are; in such places we feel more alive, more grounded, more human. If you have ventured off on a narrow pathway through the wilderness, you know how transformative the experience can be. The trail becomes a portal for exploration and self-exploration, an inward and an outward journey, a place to lose oneself and a place to find oneself. Surrounded by towering peaks, spellbound by magnificent vistas, enraptured by the natural world's stunning beauty, we melt into the landscape and become one with something grander.

Trails come in endless varieties, each providing a particular nuance and emotional resonance. Some trails cut through thick forest, earthy and damp, the smells of pine and juniper heavy in the air. Other trails are arid and exposed, lined with chaparral and coyote brush, bathed in warm sunlight and radiant energy. Each trail is a unique experience, one that leaves an indelible impression on its followers. We recall what if feels like because it affects us so intimately; the trail stays with us, inside us, like a warm glow.

I am drawn to the trails as an escape from the manufactured world we occupy. Some of us refuse to become fully domesticated and seek wild places as a refuge from humanity's trappings. Out on a trail, the world is vast and open and unpaved, the elements untamed, often savage, and we feel the fear and exhilaration of an incoming storm with our senses and in our hearts. Although we are smaller in nature, life becomes larger. Slipping away on a trail through the wilderness stirs the soul in a way few other things in life can. When we emerge from our wanderings, we are renewed and reborn and left in a state of contented bliss where all seems right.

When I'm not running on trails, I enjoy looking at images of others out in the wilds. I get inspired and energized seeing pictures of athletes in exotic places and feel a connection with the trail-running community. *Running Wild* put me alongside my trail-running compatriots on the trails in faraway locations, giving me that familiar tingle I feel whenever I'm off on a trail myself. Filled with striking imagery and vibrant illustrations, along with compelling narrative, the book had me captivated from page one. Whether you've run great distances on a trail, modest distances, or are just starting out, *Running Wild* is sure to captivate your spirit the way it did mine. Enjoy this magnificent work of artistry; let it awaken your emotions. Then, please, find a trail and get lost ...

← Trail running gives you the chance to immerse yourself in nature, such as here in British Columbia.

↑ Into the mineral worlds of Corsica, France.

→ Out on the trails, you can capture amazing moments; for example, a perfect sunrise in the White Mountains, USA.

INTRODUCTION

Whether you are gently drifting along a perfect trail weaving through a quiet forest, climbing the sides of a mountain with ragged breath and burning legs, coasting along the banks of a rushing river or pushing over dunes as you cross a desert, it's possible to experience a sense of magic as you run. This magic comes from seeing a tiny glimpse of the vastness and bewildering complexity of the natural world.

That is often the allure of the trails: the opportunity to immerse yourself in nature and feel at one with the environment. This is one of the reasons why we run. And it is one of the most compelling.

Trail running – which really is no more than running on natural surfaces, not road – is, at heart, a simple activity. It is often just a matter of picking a location, deciding on a route, packing a few essentials and setting out.

It's easy to see trail running as a perfect canvas for exploration – both literal and figurative – as well as for self-expression. And that is partly because, as alluded to earlier, there is so much variety available. Reading this collection of stories from trails around the world, you will be transported to an enormous range of different places, from hot and dry plains to cool mountains to lush forests. There is something for everyone; or perhaps everywhere is for everyone – you decide.

First and foremost, this book aims to provide inspiration. When we co-founded *Like the Wind* magazine in 2014, the idea was to collect stories that inspire, motivate and move our readers. We started out with a motto: *it's why we run*. And we stick to that idea to this day, in every quarterly issue of the journal. This book is an extension of what we have worked to create with *Like the Wind* magazine – so as well as a guide to some amazing places to run, we want to provide a huge dose of inspiration. What we hope to do is to fire up your passion to get out and explore; it may be that after reading this book, you go and run somewhere we haven't featured. We just really want you to find your way on to the trails, wherever that may be.

While the focus of this book is to inspire more people to run off-road, we do that with a very, very important caveat. Many of the most beautiful and inspiring parts of the planet are also the most fragile, both environmentally and culturally. Throughout this book, we want to emphasize that we all have a duty of care to the places in which we choose to run. The environment is under pressure in too many ways, and we hope that readers will do everything they can to preserve the flora and fauna that they encounter while running. Because without protecting the environment, we will not leave beauty and wonder for the next generation of trail runners to enjoy.

The same goes for the communities that runners encounter along the way. Almost without exception, considerate trail runners are welcomed by the people who live in these locations. We have a duty to ensure that we repay the welcome we receive with respect for local customs, religions, beliefs and cultures. Probably the best way to do that is to take time to become immersed in the way of life of the people and places along each route.

The importance of local culture and customs is part of the reason each chapter has been written by someone with a true personal connection to the area they are describing. Our guides are trail runners who know the locality either because they live (or have lived) there, or because they have had the chance to spend time on the trails. This allows you to get a sense of the geography and culture first-hand. Of course, many of the writers will happily admit that even if they have lived in the place they are writing about for years, they have yet to experience everything their location has to offer. But they are the best people we know to give you the inside information that will inspire you – as well as ensure that if you do visit the places in this book, you have the best possible experience.

We sincerely hope that *Running Wild* motivates, inspires and enables you to discover some amazing trails, whether you are a new or experienced trail runner. If you get to travel to one of the locations we have featured – or are inspired to get off-road somewhere else – we encourage you to take your time. Enjoy the nature and the people you encounter. Take in all the sensations that come your way. It is not complicated – you just need to pick a destination, pack what you need, pull on your trainers and go.

↓ Moody light along the Sunshine Coast, British Columbia, Canada.

↑ Among the giants near the Grand Canyon in Sedona, Arizona, USA.

↓ Running the cliffs in Pertusato, South Corsica - the French island of contrasts.

THE DOLOMITES

01 | ITALY: EUROPE

The Dolomites — Italy

DON'T UNDERESTIMATE THE DOLOMITES

DAVIDE GRAZIELLI

The range may not be as big as the Central Alps, but its valleys, lakes and waterfalls provide more than enough challenge and beauty

The Dolomites, sometimes referred to as the Pale Mountains, could be thought of as the Italian children of the much bigger Central Alps, up against which they nestle. Located in the north-west of Italy, the Dolomites run from the Adige River at the western extent to the Piave Valley in the east. But although this mountain range might be somewhat overshadowed by its parents, do not underestimate it. There is beauty, challenge and adventure aplenty in this corner of Italy.

The Dolomites are criss-crossed by trails, a great deal of them extremely well marked and signposted. One way of seeing many of the most beautiful parts of the area is to embark on a 120km (75½mi) journey that follows the route of the Lavaredo Ultra Trail – an epic trail race – over three or four days. The Lavaredo is considered to be one of the premier ultra-trail events in the world.

The route starts and finishes in Cortina d'Ampezzo, a town of around 6,000 inhabitants, sitting at the head of the Valle del Boite in the heart of the Dolomites. The region has had a chequered history, having been part of the Austrian Empire before Napoleon annexed the area. Nowadays, Cortina is famous for its winter sports, having hosted the 1956 Winter Olympics and been selected to co-host the 2026 Winter Games with Milan. But while the snow and all its associated activities drive the economy of the town, it is during the brief but often glorious summer that the trails promise a running paradise.

The start of the run, leaving Cortina, is the least beautiful part of the adventure. But really, this is relative – the whole place is a sight to behold and this section is about the anticipation of the wonderful areas to come. Head north out of town following the Via del Castello until you see the Cadin di Sopra on the left. Take this path and follow the signs for Passo Pospòrcora. As soon as

→ The majestic, rugged beauty of the Dolomites at Passo Giau.

↑ The climb to Forcella Lavaredo on day two represents the high point of the route.

→ (Opposite left): The Tre Cime di Lavaredo silhouetted just before sunrise.

→ (Opposite right): Running at dawn in the mineral landscapes of the Dolomites is a spectacular experience.

you leave the main road, you'll cross the river and pass a church – the Chiesa della Beata Vergine della Salute – on the left. Keep going as you pass Lago Ghedina, a small but beautiful lake surrounded by trees, and then the trail leads into the switchbacks that mark the start of the climb up towards Passo Pospòrcora – the first test for the legs.

The path winds up to the Passo Pospòrcora and then takes a sharp turn on a downhill technical trail that leads to the bottom of the valley again, towards Podestagno. The path is wide and runnable up to Ospitale; follow the signs on the right towards Rifugio son Forca, circumnavigating the imposing craggy peak of Pomagagnon. Keep following signs as you round Pomagagnon towards the Rifugio son Forca, which will come into view up the trail to your left. The scenic refuge lies at the foot of Monte Cristallo (to the east) at 2,200m (7,200ft) above sea level. As you'll reach it around halfway through the day, it's an ideal stop for lunch. From here, stick to the path as you descend to the Passo Tre Croci through forested trails, crossing the river before reaching the valley floor. Just before crossing the SR48 road, you have the option to cut your day short by

3.5km (2mi) and 400m (1,300ft) elevation by following the trail to your left. For the full day, keep going east and tackle the last climb up through the trees, where the trail continues to wind east and then turns sharply north, heading for the Lago di Misurina, our destination at 42km (26mi). High up at 1,754m (5,700ft) above sea level, the charming lake town is popular with tourists, so there are plenty of hotel and restaurant options – or you can keep pushing for the quieter Rifugio Antorno, 2.5km (1½mi) further up.

Day two starts with a superb target: the Tre Cime di Lavaredo, a group of three imposing peaks that top out at 3,000m (9,840ft) above sea level. Follow the trail up towards Rifugio Auronzo, which you'll reach after 7km (4⅓mi). From there, you start a sublime circumnavigation of the three peaks, which sit majestically on your left. Pass the Rifugio Lavaredo and you soon reach Forcella Lavaredo, the high point of the full tour. You can now enjoy some welcome downhill, through the Val della Riénza towards the Lago di Landro. On each side of the valley are walls of mountains – on your left to the south you'll see the back of the Tre Cime di Lavaredo, the Croda de l'Arghena and Monte Piano; to your right, Monte Rudo. After lunch at Lago di Landro, keep following the path along the road, then just before Lago Bianco, go straight ahead through the forest towards the Passo Cimabanche. This forest road will take you steadily uphill for 5km (3mi) alongside the foot of the Croda Rossa, a famous climbing spot in the Dolomites. This section of the route is extremely scenic and feels very remote. There is little noise and you will feel as though you are truly in the heart of the mountains. The path now climbs to Forcella Lerosa, before starting to descend into Malga Ra Stua, where the white-painted refuge sitting proudly atop the pasture is a great option for your second night on the trail.

The Lavaredo is considered to be one of the premier ultra-trail events in the world

↑ Grandiose views of the valley from above Rifugio Auronzo on day two.

With almost 50km (30mi) and 3,000m (9,800ft) elevation gain, day three can easily be split into two. Start by following the trail south towards Casón de Antruiles for the next 15km (9mi), along the Val Travenanzes – a desolate valley, with dozens of waterfalls on either side. The path follows the river as you steadily gain altitude, with the first section being very runnable before becoming covered in boulders, just before a sharp climb up to a pass. Despite the effort, remember to take in the views – the almost vertical rock faces to either side add to the brooding feel of this section of the trail. It's also worth noting that this part of the run offers nothing in the way of refuges, water stops or anywhere to get help – so stock up on water and food at Malga Ra Stua. After 12km (7½mi) of the Val Travenanzes you will reach Forcella Col dei Bos, after which you drop down to the Col Gallina, where you can eat. From Col Gallina, it is worth looking back at the way you came, up to the rock formations at the Cima Falzarego, before continuing along the trail, climbing towards the Rifugio Averau, at 23km (14mi) an ideal stop for the night if you're doing the tour in four days. The refuge offers a stunning view of the Cinque Torri, or Five Towers – a set of rock spires reaching up into the sky, which attract many climbers during the summer. For your final leg, head down south towards the Passo Giau. This section of the trail includes some areas where you have to cross big rocks strewn on the mountainside, so take care. After a few kilometres the trail reaches Forcella Ambrizzola, where it turns sharply to the left, heading north again. This is the final stretch of the route back to Cortina and so the last section to be savoured. Follow the trail past the Croda da Lago to your left. In the shadow of the Croda da Lago you will find a number of *rifugi* (refuges) – ideal for a lunch stop before you push on to Cortina. From the Croda da Lago, the run into Cortina is simple – there is a final climb up to Pocol and then it's downhill all the way back to where you started.

While the snow and all its associated activities drive the economy of the town, it is during the brief but often glorious summer that the trails promise a running paradise

← The Lavaredo Ultra Trail race starts at 11.00pm, which makes for exciting night running.

→ (Opposite above): One of the more technical stretches of the route, near Passo Giau.

→ (Right): The jagged, unmistakable Dolomite peaks near Rifugio Lavaredo.

→ (Right): On the way down from Passo Giau the boulders disappear and are replaced by vegetation.

→ (Opposite): Don't forget to turn back and check the view after passing the Tre Cime di Lavaredo.

↓ The section between the Auronzo and Lavaredo refuges offers breathtaking views of the valley.

I discovered the Dolomites in my thirties, when I dedicated myself to tackling some of the most iconic trail races in the world. One of them was the Lavaredo Ultra Trail. I vividly remember arriving in Cortina for the first time and, on seeing the amazing landscape of the mountains there, realizing that I'd been missing out for many years. Now I make sure to drive north from where I live in Italy to run in the Dolomites at least a couple of times each year, because I believe this is a unique place to run, whether in a race or simply out enjoying the trails with friends.

DAVIDE GRAZIELLI

Davide Grazielli was first introduced to trail running by his father, who raced up and down the mountains in his native Italy during the 1970s. Pretty soon Davide was running during the summer as a means to stay fit for his main sport - cross-country skiing. However, once he reached his teenage years, surfing, skating and snowboarding had much more appeal than running and skiing. In his thirties, Davide was reintroduced to trail running by some friends, and he quickly progressed to tackling 160km (100mi) races - which have become his obsession. Balancing training with a job as a lecturer at Milan University and his coaching business has not always been easy, but Davide has still managed to finish in the top twenty in the Western States 100 and the top thirty in the Ultra-Trail du Mont-Blanc. He's never far away from a trail nowadays and still competes whenever possible.

PRACTICAL INFORMATION

The Dolomites, like many mountainous areas in central Europe, are criss-crossed by well-maintained trails and are generally well signposted. However, in some of the more remote parts of the area around Lavaredo, the signposts are few and far between. Make sure you take a careful note of the directions you should follow; then there is little chance of getting lost. Of course, the Dolomites are proper mountains and all the usual precautions should be taken – although it should be said that by European Alpine standards, the route described here is not particularly technical.

The accommodation in the mountains – in the form of mountain refuges, known as *rifugi* – is plentiful and generally of a very high standard (although, as with the town of Cortina, it is not cheap). The *rifugi* are privately owned and almost universally offer dinner, bed and breakfast to the weary runner, as well as everything else a runner needs, so all you'll really have to pack is a toothbrush and a sleeping bag liner. You are usually able to order a packed lunch for the following day, although as you pass *rifugi* during the day, it is possible – even advisable – to stop at one for lunch. Be sure to book overnight accommodation in advance; *rifugi* will get very busy, especially at the height of the summer season. Many have their own websites.

APPROX. DISTANCE	120km (74½mi)	MAXIMUM ALTITUDE	2,450m (8,040ft)	CLIMATE	Alpine: 20-25°C (68-77°F) in summer, but colder the higher you go	TERRAIN	forest, rocks
APPROX. ELEVATION	5,800m (19,000ft)	SEASON TO RUN	June-Sept	CHALLENGE LEVEL	advanced	WATCH OUT FOR	signposts can be few and far between; unpredictable weather; residual snow

TRE CIME DI LAVAREDO

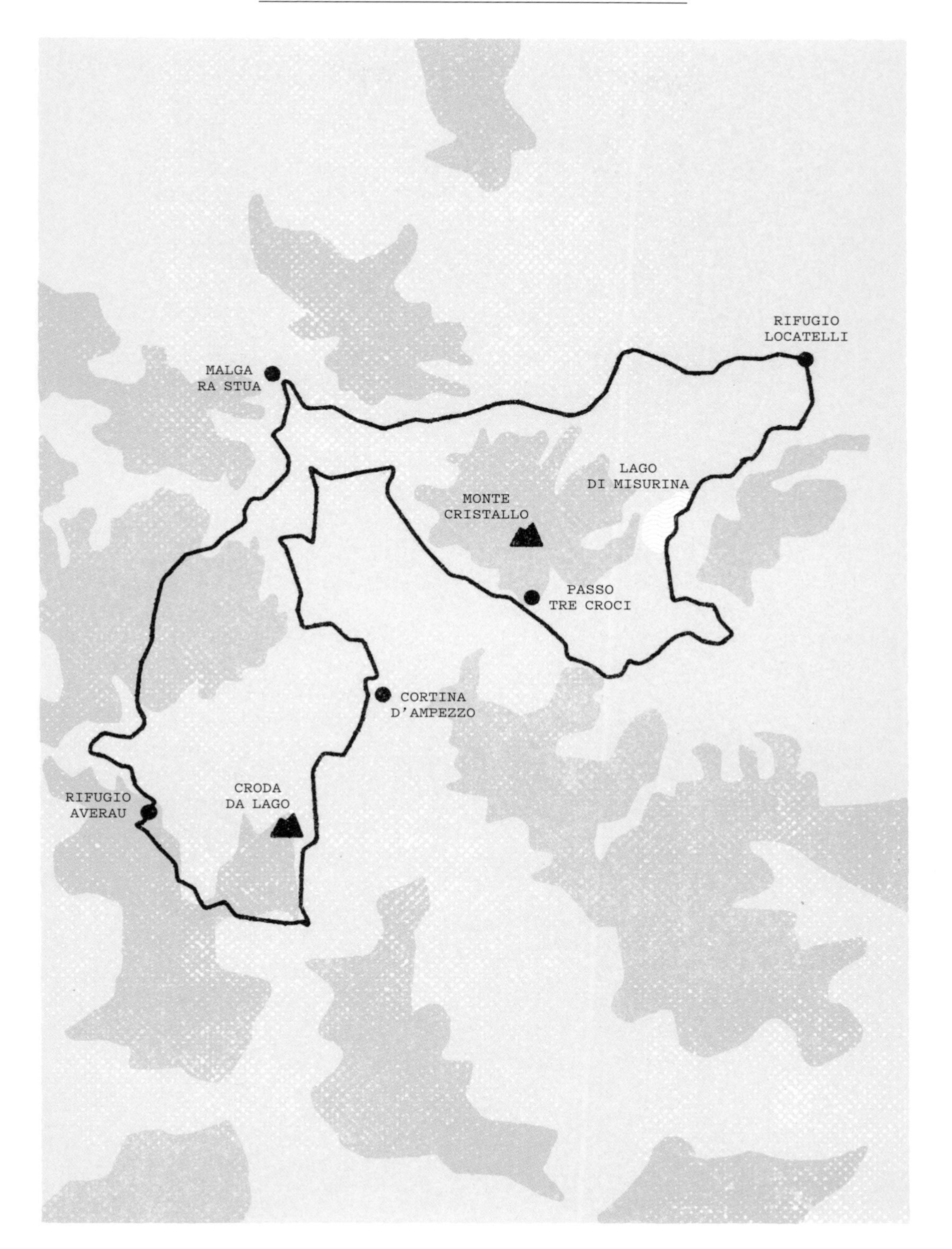

THE LOFOTEN ISLANDS

02 | NORWAY: EUROPE

The Lofoten Islands — Norway

THE MAGIC OF THE MIDNIGHT SUN

LINDA HELLAND

Months of twenty-four-hour daylight bring an ethereal feel to the dark fjords and granite peaks of these mountainous islands off the northern coast of Norway

The ferry to Værøy island leaves Bodø at 5.30am. On a clear summer day, the shining sun bathes the islands outside the harbour in a warm morning light. Værøy is located above the Arctic Circle, the second-outermost inhabited island of the archipelago of Lofoten. Though the climate is rough, making all kinds of weather possible, Værøy also offers twenty-four hours of daylight during the summer: runners who visit between late May and mid-July will experience the magic of the midnight sun.

Lofoten consists of several islands off the mainland of northern Norway. The area's characteristic mountains rise straight from the ocean – seen from the mainland, the apparent straight line formed by their peaks is called the Lofoten Wall. The running possibilities are endless, especially if ascents are your cup of tea. While you are still more likely to meet hikers on the trails, trail running is picking up. For runners after a real challenge, Lofoten Ultra-Trail has become an annual event, part of the Arctic Triple, while the Lofoten Skyrace features a vertical challenge.

The season of the midnight sun offers some outstanding views. If the weather is good, follow Værøy's most popular trail and see the iconic panorama from the summit, Håen. Reaching Håen can involve a short and fairly easy run (around a 7.5km/4½mi round trip if running via Hornet), or it can form part of the full circumnavigation, around 25–30km (15½–18½mi) depending on the route, covering all the summits and trails of the island.

→ The Lofoten Ultra-Trail offers a unique geographical challenge.

The route gains elevation quickly, zig-zagging on soft trails to reach the first peak, Hornet, at 346m (1,135ft). At Hornet, the trail faces the rough north-west side of the island: the cliff drops directly into the dark blue ocean. From here, the ridge run towards Håen (438m/1,437ft) is amazing. The trail stays on the safe side – however, it offers multiple opportunities to take in the views. It's not unusual to encounter fog, but as it lifts it gradually reveals the view that visitors long for: the waves hitting the white beach sheltered by the mountain and the tiny, now-deserted village of Måstad, with Værøy's southernmost summit, Måhornet, in the background.

The area's characteristic mountains rise straight from the ocean – seen from the mainland, the apparent straight line formed by their peaks is called the Lofoten Wall

The climb to Måhornet begins on the beautiful beach at Nordlandshagen, on the north side of the island. The initial 6km (3¾mi) of the trail hugs the shoreline and features very little elevation before the ascent to Måhornet. But it's not easy: the first 4km (2½mi) is technical, although as you cross over a small pass from the north to the south shore, it gets better, featuring an unfinished road, intended to connect the people of Måstad to the rest of Værøy.

Leaving Måstad, the trail gets super-narrow and steep as the climb towards Måhornet (439m/1,440ft) begins. Your approach to the summit may well be supervised by a sea eagle circling above. While the view from Håen is legendary, looking towards Håen is no less spectacular.

An amazing spot to watch the fabled midnight sun hovering over the ocean is the summit of Nordlandsnupen. Nordlandsnupen remains relatively unknown, although everything about this short summit run (4km/2½mi up and down to a 450m/1,476ft peak) is perfect, from the tropical-ish beach at the trailhead to

the soft trails and incredible views at the pass halfway, including a few exposed parts, before hitting the even better 360-degree vista at the top.

On the descent from Nordlandsnupen, you'll pass the trail to Hornet. From here, it's possible to see how all the trails and summits of the island are connected. A complete island run could cover the summits of Måtind, Håen, Hornet and Nordlandsnupen in one go.

Lofoten is equally spectacular during the autumn. The midnight sun and seasonal crowds are swapped for golden autumnal colours and the possibility of a full night's sleep before sunrise. The run to watch the sun come up at Reinebringen, on the island of Moskenesøya, is highly recommended. The route begins at the Sherpa steps, which will get the heart rate up and thighs burning, although the surroundings are insanely beautiful. The autumn colours pop, divided from the ocean only by the road that perfectly follows the coast, while everything around is bathed in a mysterious soft lilac morning light. It takes some 1,566 steps to reach the top; this is a run like no other.

Reinebringen's beauty is breathtaking – its fairytale-like view of dark fjords and lakes is surrounded by the dramatic landscape of never-ending pointed granite mountains. But Reinebringen doesn't have to be your final destination.

← (Left): Breathtaking vistas from the iconic Håen viewpoint on Værøy.

← (Right): A final scramble brings you to the summit of Reinetoppen.

↓ A lone competitor takes on the Lofoten Ultra-Trail.

↑ The Lofoten Ultra-Trail takes place in June, though there is still snow on the ground.

↑ One of the classic Reinebringen viewpoints.

→ You'll be sharing the trails with hikers, and maybe local wildlife, too.

→ (Opposite): Granite mountains create a truly dramatic landscape.

Follow the ridge that passes Reinetoppen – and crosses an area called 'hell' – to reach the summit with no name other than 'Topp 730'.

The unmarked trail along the ridge is easy to follow, though not always easy to conquer. 'Hell' is partly soft, partly soil, partly mountain rock. At some points runners may find themselves crawling on all fours; at others, you may need the support of a fellow runner. It can take several hours to cover the 3.5km (2mi) to the 645m (2,116ft) Reine summit, but you will have conquered 'hell'. After a small descent, the trail passes through a soft, golden meadow on the way up to Topp 730.

Lofoten is equally spectacular during the autumn. The midnight sun and seasonal crowds are swapped for golden autumnal colours and the possibility of a full night's sleep before sunrise

The first section of the descent from Topp 730 leads back through the same meadow to the trail that brings you down from the Reine summit. Turning right towards Austerdalsvatnet and then Djupfjorden represents the start of a technical, sometimes wet descent that does not make for an easy run. However, this is compensated for by the view of the dark granite wall formed by Munken mountain and its siblings on the other side of Austerdalsvatnet. An alternative route retraces the trail from the way up, offering the chance of a detour to the beautiful Austerdalsvatnet trail.

↓ The Lofoten Ultra-Trail is as brutal as it is beautiful.

↓ (Below): Traditional red boat-storage houses (*naust*), typical of the region.

↑ The rough climate makes all kinds of weather possible, even during summer.

← The season of the midnight sun offers some outstanding views.

↑ Most visitors to the trails are hikers, but trail running is becoming more popular.

→ Heading further north along the coast reveals yet another side of the Lofoten Islands.

Although many years have passed since the childhood summers I spent in the northern part of Norway, heading north always feels like going home. Up north, there isn't space for much more than nature. Your mind is at rest while your body moves along the tiny ground left between the ocean and the dark grey granite walls.

The wind touches your face, bringing so much peace. It gives me a sense of connection, not only to nature, but also to my father, who passed away before I got to know him. When I'm in Lofoten, I try to picture how my father must have felt about this place. He was a fisherman during the 1960s, and would have worked through some truly harsh winters. The first time I visited, I was a tourist, in my twenties, staying in old-fashioned fishermen's cabins and experiencing for the first time the unique landscape of Lofoten – even though the islands are only a ferry trip and a couple of hours' drive from where I spent my childhood summers.

Tales of my father running up the backyard mountains and memories of him swimming in the ocean have always inspired me to seek the quietness of the outdoors and added that extra spring to my step.

→ If the uphill doesn't take your breath away, the view from Himmeltinden on Vestvågøy island certainly will.

MEET THE GUIDE

LINDA HELLAND

As a cross-country skier in the winter and a trail runner during the summer, Linda Helland's passion for the outdoors has taken her on numerous adventures in her home country, Norway, as well as abroad, where the Swiss Alps and the Dolomites are among her favourite destinations. While Linda has participated in many of the big trail-running events, such as the Matterhorn Ultraks in Zermatt, the Swissalpine marathon in Davos and the Tromsø Skyrace in Norway, her focus has shifted towards exploring new areas and trails outside of competition, on her own or with friends.

PRACTICAL INFORMATION

The best time for trail running in Lofoten is between June and early October. Depending on where you are, the midnight sun season lasts from late May until mid-July. Tourism peaks during July and August. Note that most of the trails are more technical than those of somewhere like the Alps; you may not be able to move as fast as you usually do.

With public transport limited, you either need to rent a car or plan very carefully how to reach your desired destinations. By flying into Bodø and taking the ferry to Værøy and later on to Moskenes, you can manage without a car. It can be worth booking accommodation and ferry tickets as much as six months in advance. Værøy is not the place to go on a whim.

Visitors to Værøy can stay in hotel rooms or apartments at modern fishermen's lodges. The beachside campsite at Nordlandshagen has running water and a toilet. It's also perhaps the best starting point for a complete island trail experience. Check the weather forecast to ensure you get the best views. If you're tackling Nordlandsnupen, try to wait until the cloud clears before you hit the trail.

The minimum height for 'hell' to Topp 730 is around 160cm (5ft 2in), unless you have support. The few obstacles are not exposed and can be managed if you are experienced in the mountains. It also helps to run as a pair. The 2km (1¼mi) fjord trail (an optional part of the descent from Topp 730) is technical; during autumn it can be wet and muddy.

As of 2021, wild camping is illegal during the summer in parts of Lofoten, including the area around Reinebringen. Plan ahead, seek advice from local tourist information, be mindful of the surrounding landscape and – most importantly – leave no trace.

APPROX. DISTANCE	50km (30mi)	MAXIMUM ALTITUDE	645m (2,116ft)	CLIMATE	Oceanic: around 13°C (55°F) in summer	TERRAIN	occasionally stony; also beach and some wet sections
APPROX. ELEVATION	1,800m (5,900ft)	SEASON TO RUN	June–Oct	CHALLENGE LEVEL	mixed	WATCH OUT FOR	technical trails; fog; 'hell'

VÆRØY

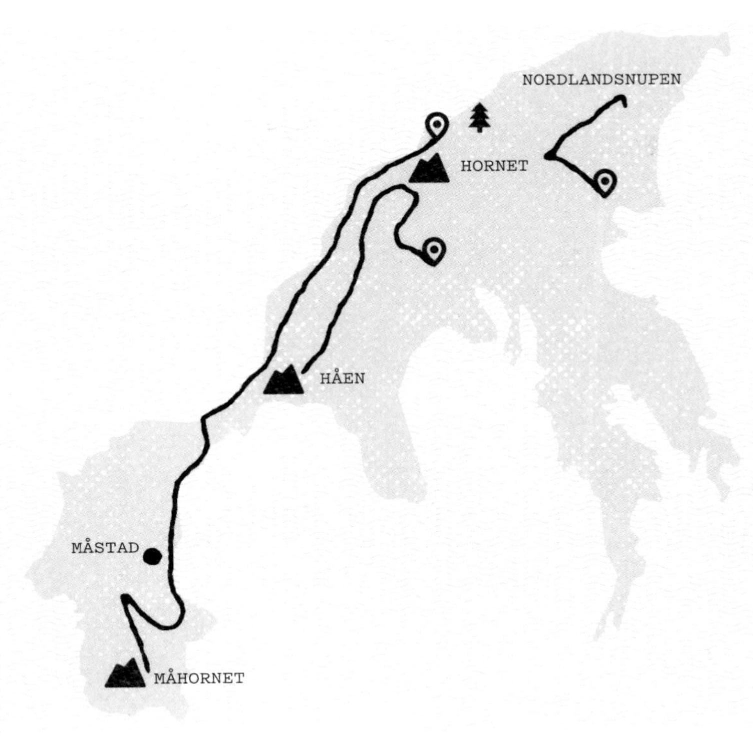

MOSKENESØYA

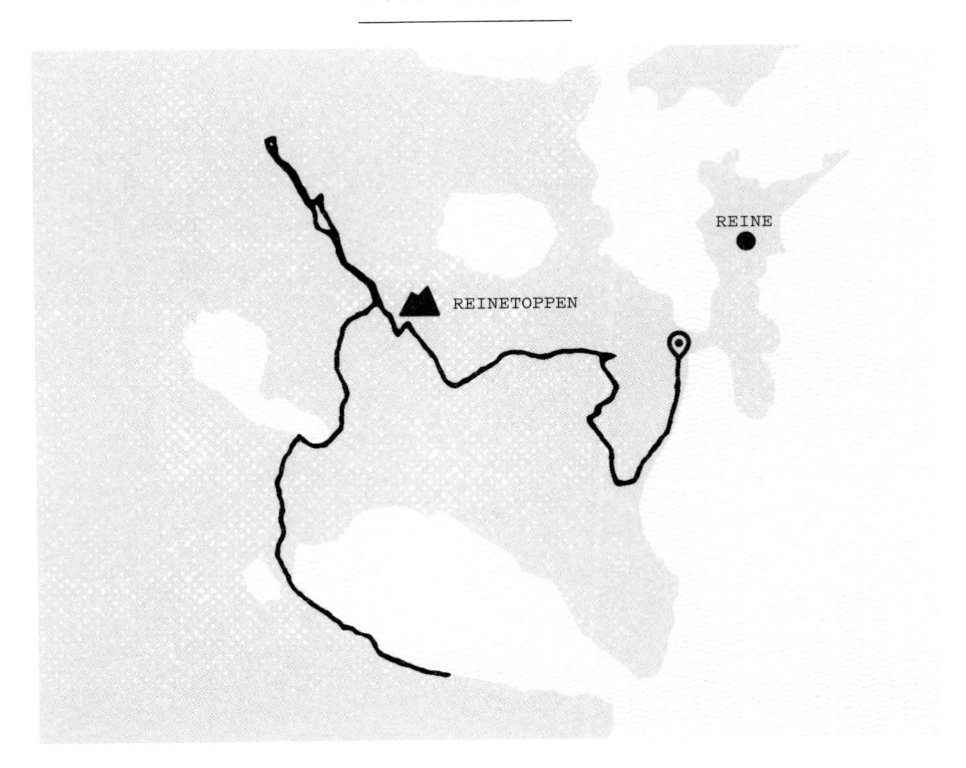

THE CHAMONIX VALLEY

03 | FRANCE: EUROPE

THE CHAMONIX VALLEY — FRANCE

The Chamonix Valley — France

UNFORGETTABLE VIEWS IN THE FRENCH ALPS

SIMON FREEMAN

On foot during the summer, the Chamonix Valley is a runner's playground, revealing its true beauty and variety – which makes it perfect for exploring the Alps

← On the trail up to Lac Blanc from the Col des Montets, on the Grand Balcon Sud.

Towering above the Chamonix Valley at an altitude of 4,810m (15,780ft), the majestic Mont Blanc is the jewel in the Alps' crown, a sight that has been taking people's breath away for centuries. Its uniqueness and cultural importance make it the birthplace and symbol of modern mountaineering.

When nineteenth-century British climbers started flocking to the French Alpine town, they slowly elevated what had been a sleepy area to a bustling hotspot of all things mountain. Today, the number of people in Chamonix swells from fewer than 10,000 to more than 60,000 at the height of the winter ski season. It's easy to feel a bit blasé about Chamonix, with its cable cars, funiculars and elevators making short work of the peaks and bringing even the most under-prepared to the top of Europe with minimal effort. Yet it's on foot that the Chamonix Valley reveals its true beauty – and when the winter sports enthusiasts have packed away their skis, the summer is the perfect time for runners to explore its wonders.

Until the late eighteenth century, the Chamonix Valley and its surroundings were part of the Duchy of Savoy, an independent state with a mostly French culture stretching from the south shore of Lake Geneva in Switzerland to Genoa in Italy. Today, with the duchy dissolved and the ownership of Mont Blanc split between France and Italy, the French influence is still felt on either side of the mountain. A few common traditions reach all the way to Switzerland, including the practice of cow-fighting – which exploits the natural behaviour of cattle battling each other (with blunted horns) to determine dominance in the herd.

Clutching the sides of the glacial Arve River, sixteen villages form the commune of Chamonix-Mont-Blanc, stretching 23km (14mi) from Le Tour to Les Bossons. The two Petit Balcon trails, Nord (north) and Sud (south), traverse the sides of the valley at low altitude (about 1,200–1,500m/3,900–5,000ft), while their big brothers, the Grands Balcons Nord and Sud, run in parallel at about 2,000m (6,560ft). In between, myriad trails criss-cross both sides of the valley, stretching into neighbouring valleys and even to Italy and Switzerland. Those trails are perfect for day runs, because it's relatively quick to get back down to the comfort and safety of the valley floor (either on foot or by cable car).

A suspended bridge above a glacial torrent offers glimpses of the wonders to come

The steepness of the valley walls means that it is possible to run what is technically called a 'vertical kilometre' – a 1,000m (3,280ft) ascent over a route of only 3.8km (2⅓mi). On such vertigo-inducing trails, even experienced trail runners agree that power-hiking can be more efficient than running. The steepness and technicality of the trails around Mont Blanc mean that a lot of the terrain is not, in the strictest sense, readily runnable. In some ways, this is a godsend: it provides an excuse to slow down, hike up and enjoy the scenery.

All along the valley, and far up its hillsides and peaks, charming refuges (originally established to provide basic amenities to mountaineers) are welcome stops for runners and hikers to take food, drink and shelter. Situated every

← Some technical – but not difficult – features on the final few hundred metres leading up to the Lac Blanc refuge.

↓ Lac Blanc, with its glacial waters – a perfect mirror for Mont Blanc, which towers on the opposite side of the valley.

10–15km (6–9mi), these Alpine oases are perfect lunch destinations or shelter for a night to remember. Each refuge has its own character: accommodation ranges from small rooms to basic dormitories and various levels of bathroom luxury. Refuges will typically serve a hearty meal at 7.00pm sharp on long communal tables. Don't expect deep sleep, but that's all the better to prepare you for the multi-day races that are popular here.

An excellent way to get acquainted with the Chamonix Valley is to follow the gentle trails of the Petit Balcon Nord or Sud. In the shadow of pine forests, the ground is soft underfoot, with few rocks and roots. Further up, above the treeline, the trails narrow and larger rocks make running more technical, with larger boulder fields and steep scree slopes.

Once you're ready for more – and for some truly unforgettable views – head to the Grand Balcon Nord or Sud and follow the trail from Chamonix all the way to the Col des Montets. From here, the stunning high lakes trail leads up to the Lac Blanc, a great place to spend the night. There are some seriously technical passages during this climb, including sections of small metal ladders permanently affixed to the steep rocks. On the way down, the Sentier des Gardes offers a wild ride all the way back to the valley: a gloriously uninterrupted downhill run that can last several hours.

For more practised runners, a multi-day trip along the Tour du Mont Blanc (TMB) trail is an incredible Alpine adventure providing memories that will last

← Both the Grand Balcons (Nord and Sud) are just above the treeline, traversing meadows dotted with ponds and blueberry bushes.

← (Opposite below): July to September are the calmest seasons to visit Chamonix, but even if you set off under perfect blue skies, surprise afternoon storms can be fierce.

a lifetime (and may even make you sign up for *that* race around Mont Blanc). The TMB passes through France, Italy and Switzerland over 160km (100mi) of well-marked trails featuring numerous refuges.

From Chamonix, head to Les Houches and up to the Col du Tricot via Bellevue (it makes sense to take the cable car – this part of the trail isn't super-interesting). A suspended bridge above a glacial torrent offers glimpses of the wonders to come. There's not much running to be done on the way up, as the Col du Tricot is a steep affair, but the promise of a cold beverage at the Col du Miage should keep you power-hiking. Before Les Contamines, you can veer off the TMB route and follow signs to the Refuge de Tré-la-Tête, where the route up follows exposed rocky trails above the Contamines Valley. The refuge might be perfect for lunch, or even to stay the night.

What goes up must come down. An epic technical trail, with rocky, stairlike sections, leads back down the valley before the start of the Col du Bonhomme and on to the Col de la Croix du Bonhomme at 2,432m (7,979ft). At times, these ascents seem interminable. However, the refuge at the Col de la Croix du Bonhomme may offer the best night's sleep imaginable. (From Bellevue it's 25km/15½mi and a 2,560m/8,400ft ascent, which takes more than nine hours as a hike, but six when mixing running and power-hiking.)

A useful principle works all around the TMB: splitting days between huts. 'Single' (10–12km/6–7½mi) or 'double' days (18–25km/11–15½mi, with one hut for lunch and the next for the night) make it possible to plan a route from refuge to refuge. Following this logic, you can get down to Courmayeur in another day (30km/18½mi via Chécrouit or slightly shorter via Lac Combal) or stay the night at an Italian refuge, the Rifugio Elisabetta Soldini, en route. The trail then continues across to Switzerland, via the Grand Col Ferret (where you can experience yet another style of hut and food), and back to Chamonix via the Col de la Forclaz, Vallorcine and La Flégère.

What goes up must come down. An epic technical trail, with rocky, stairlike sections, leads back down the valley before the start of the Col du Bonhomme

Along the way, remember the hardy souls who, at the end of every August, attempt to run the whole of the TMB in one go, in less than forty-four hours. Sometimes, during their second night, the participants in the Ultra-Trail du Mont-Blanc (UTMB) might look up to a perfect Milky Way and recall the first time they came to walk those same trails.

↑ Another view from Lac Blanc, high above the Grand Balcon Sud, with Mont Blanc in the background.

← (Opposite left): The Tour du Mont Blanc crosses many glacial streams and torrents, especially early in the season when the snow melts.

← (Opposite right): Tackling the 'Vertical Kilometre' from Le Brévent cable car station is a popular three-hour technical hike - your reward is a stunning view of the valley.

My wife Julie and I married in Switzerland and opted for a low-key honeymoon, hiking part of the TMB route. We carefully planned a relaxed, three-day hike over 80km (50mi) ... and then the storms came and turned our trip into a two-day fastpacking adventure, making us into trail runners overnight. I had not really been aware of trail running before this – I was first and foremost a road runner, and to me all mountain runners had to be elite athletes.

It was only when we were forced to cover 80km (50mi) over two days that I realized how small the gap between hiking and trail running was. Julie and I were carrying sizeable backpacks and wearing hiking boots, but still we managed to run most of the flat sections and some of the less technical downhills – thereby turning a humble hike into a stunning and rewarding first trail-running experience. Our quads were absolutely trashed after the first 40km (25mi) day, but the second day was surprisingly fun, even on tired legs.

← Despite the Tour du Mont Blanc trail's popularity, it's still possible to find peace and quiet.

→ The Sentier des Gardes, one of the most beautiful, less-trodden trails of the Chamonix Valley.

SIMON FREEMAN

Simon Freeman, born and bred in London, started running as an antidote to an unhealthy lifestyle. Before long he set his sights on completing a marathon, which turned into an obsession that came to dominate his life for many years. After co-founding *Like the Wind* with his wife Julie, Simon decided to expand his running horizons and took to the trails, participating in many races, including two finishes at the UTMB CCC (Courmayeur-Champex-Chamonix). Now Simon spends half his time and focus on running for the love of it, the communities he's part of, and exploration; and the other half on telling running stories that inspire, motivate and entertain the readers of *Like the Wind*.

PRACTICAL INFORMATION

Chamonix takes care of its hikers – and runners – with extremely well-maintained and well-indicated trails. Yellow arrows show the next destination, often with an indication of distance or time; a fast hiker or a runner may expect to cover the distance at least 25 per cent quicker than the signs claim. Staying on track is not a problem: a multitude of white and red paint markings, on trees or stones, are there to help.

Nestled in its mountain surroundings, the Chamonix Valley presents a challenge of altitude, especially if you're not acclimatized to higher ground. The difference in oxygen levels can be felt even on the valley floor – Chamonix stands at 1,035m (3,395ft) altitude. The unmatched selection of trails (from easy to climbing-grade routes with metal ladders) means that reaching altitudes of 2,000m (6,560ft) within two hours of leaving town is not a problem. Effects of altitude include shortness of breath, which will be amplified by the effort of running.

It is not very common for people to become seriously ill at the typical cruising altitude of Alpine trails (1,500–2,500m/4,900–8,200ft), yet the risk of altitude sickness cannot be ignored. If you get a headache, start vomiting or feel dizzy, it's important that you descend to lower ground as soon as is practical. Those symptoms could indicate a more serious and potentially life-threatening case of high-altitude pulmonary edema (HAPE) or fluid in the lungs (more common above 2,500m/8,200ft).

With altitude also comes exposure to unpredictable weather. Make sure to check a specific mountain weather forecast daily for your actual altitude and area before you head out. Hotels and refuges will often be very knowledgeable about this, so don't hesitate to ask for advice.

APPROX. DISTANCE	160km (100mi)	MAXIMUM ALTITUDE	2,432m (7,979ft)	CLIMATE	Alpine: 20-25°C (68-77°F) in summer, but colder the higher you go	TERRAIN	pasture; rocky; rooty; boulders
APPROX. ELEVATION	10,000m (32,800ft)	SEASON TO RUN	June-Sept	CHALLENGE LEVEL	mixed	WATCH OUT FOR	steep ascents/ descents; limited water; unpredictable weather

TOUR DU MONT BLANC

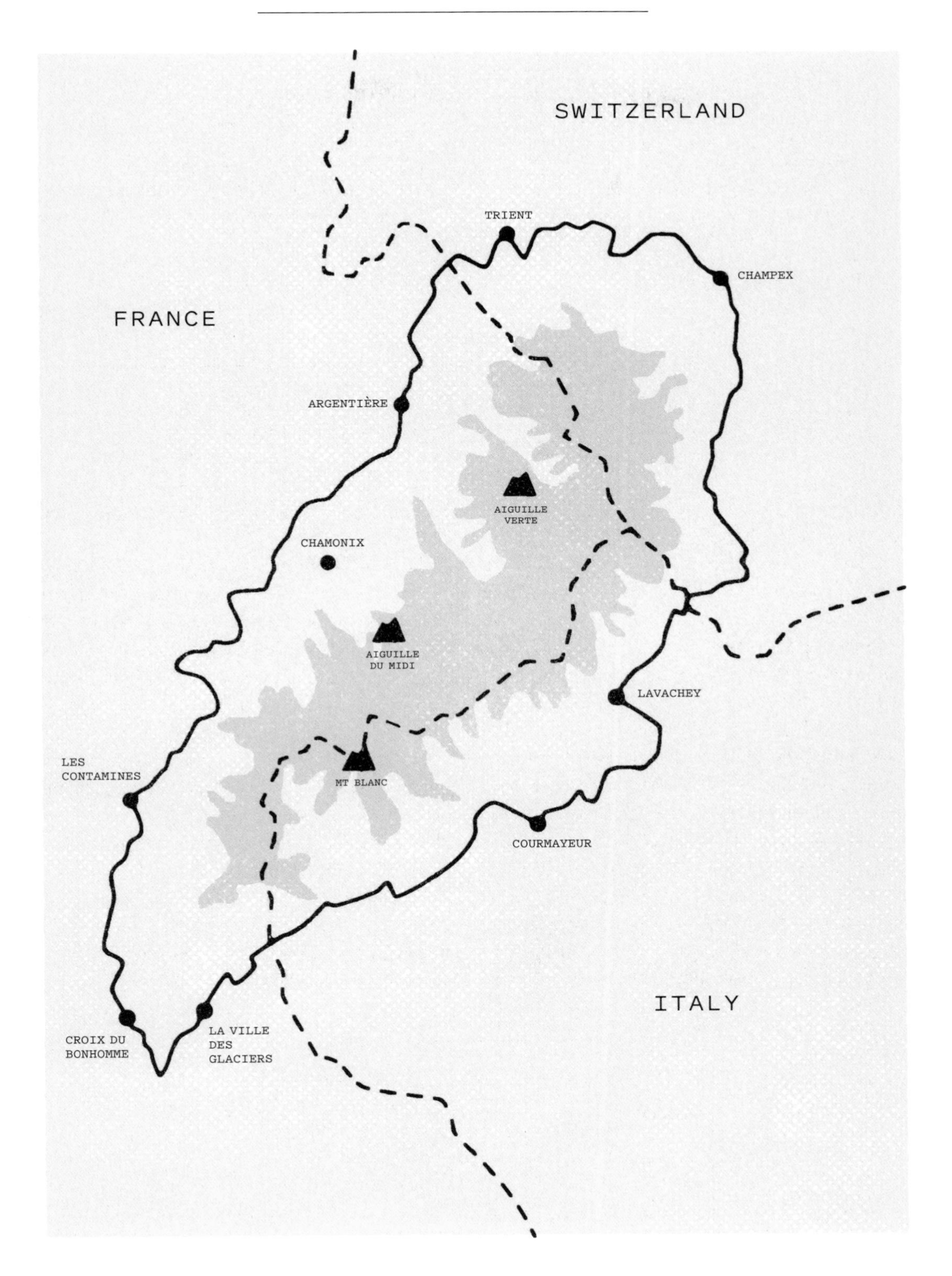

INVERIE & THE KNOYDART PENINSULA

04 | SCOTLAND: EUROPE

Inverie & The Knoydart Peninsula — Scotland

A SCOTTISH HIGHLAND LANDSCAPE SHAPED BY WATER

GEORGE BAUER

Each season brings an array of contrasting colours that highlight vast, heather-covered open spaces, winding sheep trails and craggy peaks

Knoydart has an almost mythical feel. An abundance of water brings seasons that change rapidly – the climate encourages a spring characterized by an insane variety of wildflowers and an autumn with a colour palette that shifts daily. During the summer months, the colours of the jagged peaks that have been carved out over countless seasons by rain and snow create a contrast against a sky that an artist could only dream of painting.

The Knoydart Peninsula remains one of the most remote parts of Scotland, thanks to its inaccessibility by road and sometimes harsh weather conditions. Scotland's west coast is blessed with copious rainfall, resulting in stunning lochs and rivers.

The attraction of Knoydart and nearby Glenelg is the vast open spaces covered in dense heather, winding sheep trails and craggy peaks above small villages, surrounded by beautiful Corbetts and Munros. According to the Scottish Mountaineering Club's definition of the height and size of mountains, Munros are those that rise more than 915m (3,000ft) above sea level, while Corbetts rise more than 760m (2,500ft).

Regardless of where you live, your journey to reach Knoydart will be memorable. It may involve a train trip to Mallaig, along some of the most scenic railway tracks in the world. What the final stretch to Inverie will definitely entail is either a forty-five-minute small ferry journey from Mallaig, or a three-day hike over some of Lochaber's most spectacular terrain. Cars are kept to a minimum on Knoydart, making your sturdy legs your one and only transport once you arrive.

→ Scottish photographer and trail runner Reuben Tabner exploring Knoydart, high above Loch Nevis.

Inverie is Knoydart's main village. It consists of a general store, a pub, a brand-new village hall and a local hangout known as The Table, an informal

community initiative aimed at creating a welcoming space where locals and guests can feel at home, connect with each other and share stories over a drink.

Arnisdale and Corran are two tiny villages at the end of the road on the north side of Loch Hourn. They are reached either by hiking, a wonderful scenic drive via Glenelg, or a small, private boat from Barrisdale. These small villages are an amazing base from which to explore the beautiful and rugged Glen Arnisdale and its surrounding Munros and Corbetts.

Highland cows guard the base of the hills, while plenty of wild deer make themselves at home among the dense heather high above the glens

The Knoydart area is also part of the Cape Wrath Trail, which stretches from Fort William all the way to Cape Wrath in the north of Scotland. The Cape Wrath Ultra – said to be Scotland's colder, wetter and longer version of the Marathon des Sables – provides a competition goal for many runners in the UK. Mountain running as a sport in the area is buzzing.

An amazing four-day adventure begins in Inverie – and even though the sea conditions may make the idea of an exploratory run seem uninviting, lacing up and getting out there is highly recommended. A selection of little trails around Inverie help you to find your feet, as well as providing a chance to unwind and to breathe in the fresh air. A great option is to head east towards Long Beach, for beautiful views out over Inverie Bay and the Isle of Rum in the distance. From here, there's a wonderful perspective of not only the village but also the wondrous glens (valleys) above Kilchoan Estate. Following the river leads to the estate's wee bridge. The right turn after Knoydart Lodge joins up to the Knoydart in a Knutshell loop – an expanse of trails leading back to Inverie through lush forest and over streams with beautiful clear water.

Day two is a fastpacking trip to Barrisdale Bay; very quickly you will notice few signs of human habitation among the surrounding mountains. The trail begins as a four-wheel drive track out of the forest behind Inverie, and then continues up the glen beside Inverie River. You'll find yourself in awe of the landscapes, working towards the saddle, Mam Barrisdale, which sits between Knoydart's two tallest Munros, Ladhar Bheinn and Luinne Bheinn.

Arriving alongside Loch an Dubh-Lochain (Little Black Lake), the flowing path narrows to a single track, revealing an immense view of the climb ahead reflecting off the calm waters. Underfoot, you are now hopping from rock to puddle as the boggy single track winds up to Mam Barrisdale. The saddle makes for a fabulous stop for a drink and a bite to eat, looking down the other side and back over the sparkling waters of the loch. Take three breaths here and let it soak in.

The descent is via a single track, crossing streams and endless sheep tracks. Highland cows guard the base of the hills, while wild deer make themselves at home among the dense heather high above the glens. The finishing point of the day's run is the jetty at Barrisdale Bay at the end of the track, on the beachy shores of Loch Hourn.

← Loch Nevis from Sgùrr Coire Choinnichean.

The boat from Barrisdale Bay to Arnisdale and Corran is captained by local legend Peter; it's not only the shortcut across the loch, but a chance to listen to

↑ Out on the trails, Reuben scrambles the route towards Barrisdale and drinks the freshest water imaginable.

one of the elders of the community. Peter and his family have lived in the area for many generations, and Peter has even completed a few ultra-marathons in his time.

Day three presents a new challenge, in which exploring Glen Arnisdale and climbing to the summit of Beinn nan Caorach will really showcase water and the raw beauty it creates – winding up the glen, crossing the river, passing through dense old-growth forest and finally up past the waterfall signifying the start of the Arnisdale River. From here the trail winds itself lochside before turning left up the boggy track towards the bealach (mountain pass). Depending on the time of year the path may feel more like an endless bog, but keep trudging through. Taking the first left up towards the Beinn brings the reward of a truly memorable view (imaginary or real, depending on cloud cover). All that is left is to enjoy the zig-zagging downhill section back towards the glen and on to the shores of Loch Hourn.

The final day follows the Old Coast Path along the banks of Loch Hourn – the best part being that it finishes with a rewarding hot cup of tea and home-made cake

The final day follows the Old Coast Path along the banks of Loch Hourn – the best part being that it finishes with a rewarding hot cup of tea and home-made cake. Navigation is simple, an out-and-back starting and finishing at Sheena's Tea Hut and continuing past the friendly chickens out to the pebbly beach facing Knoydart. The path undulates on to cliffs, over tree roots and back down to gravelly beaches. The track finishes at the third beach. Here the loch narrows and there's a view across to Barrisdale Bay on the other side, providing a time for reflection at the achievements of the past few days.

↑ Sunset over Loch Nevis and the Isle of Rum.

← Following the water up from Loch an Dubh-Lochain.

→ Knoydart's environment is shaped by water.

↑ On top of the world, taking in the vast majesty of the landscape.

↑ Long Beach, Inverie and Luinne Bheinn in the distance.

The Highlands – more specifically, Lochaber and Knoydart – occupy a special place in my heart. I arrived at a time when outsiders weren't overly welcome in many parts of the region: fears were rife about what Covid-19 would entail. Also, I was a cook who preferred to source and eat plants. As I tried to create menus in an area where meat plays a main role in the traditional diet, I was met with a lot of laughter. But I soon formed strong bonds with others as we discovered the accessibility of the natural world that surrounds the town and shared our common understandings of life.

As a runner who grew up in Australia, I struggled a lot at first with the Lochaber and Knoydart terrain: muddy paths that just kept disappearing into endless bog. After my initial run up a mountain, I quickly learned that coming home with soaked shoes and muddy knees was going to be a daily occurrence.

One day, as I was standing between the setting afternoon sun and the north ridge of Luinne Bheinn, the mythical nature of Knoydart came to life. The birds were singing and a family of red deer stood gazing out over the vast wilderness and the glistening lochs. It was at this moment I felt very small in this big world we live in, and considered myself very lucky to be accepted as a visitor.

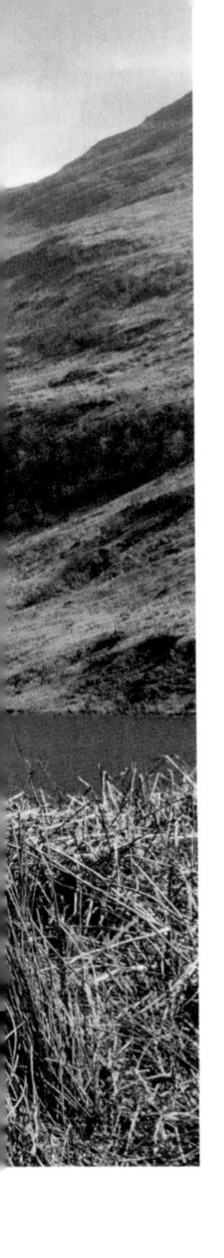

↑ The landscape creates scenes an artist could only dream of painting.

↓ Knoydart really does have an almost mythical feel.

GEORGE BAUER

Originally from Melbourne, Australia, for most of his life George Bauer called the sandy beach trails home. However, he dreamed of what it might be like to explore mountainous single-track trails from his doorstep. It was this deep curiosity, together with his Celtic heritage, that led him to end up in the Highlands of Scotland.

George works as a cook and project designer, focusing on creating community through the intersection of the two favourite areas of his life: local, seasonal produce that fuels a plant-based lifestyle, and exploring the exciting ways in which we can exercise the body and mind within nature.

He considers himself lucky to have participated in both ultra-marathons and unsanctioned events across many countries. These races and his new-found perspectives keep him motivated and inspired to run as both a form of exploration and a way of creating memorable experiences to share with others.

PRACTICAL INFORMATION

Subsistence farming is common but, as you'll notice if you arrive by ferry, many supplies are brought in by boat. Therefore, it's essential to plan your adventure well, ensuring you aren't stuck knocking on someone's door, asking them to cook you a meal. There are a handful of accommodation options to suit most budgets, alongside the beautiful houses of the local community. Research your accommodation selection: places to stay in Inverie and on the shores of Loch Hourn should ideally be booked in advance, as should Peter's boat to Arnisdale and Corran.

If you wish to support Inverie's The Table initiative as a guest in this special place, simply buy a drink from the general store and enjoy it responsibly across the street. On days three and four of the adventure outlined above, you'll spend a lot of time at Sheena's Tea Hut. Help sustain the local economy by eating out for some meals, and always aim to leave the area you visit in better condition than when you arrived.

Even though the landscape may seem inviting, take it easy on day one as you arrive in Inverie; your legs have another three days of adventure coming. Day two is just you, the wild animals and the trails, so make sure you pack enough food and water. At the end of day four, the return to civilization is via the road out towards Glenelg and Shiel Bridge. You can organize a taxi pickup from Glenelg Taxis, or there is an irregular bus service that will take you to Shiel Bridge.

APPROX. DISTANCE	40km (25mi)	MAXIMUM ALTITUDE	780m (2,560ft)	CLIMATE	rainy, occasionally harsh	TERRAIN	boggy; rocky
APPROX. ELEVATION	1,800m (5,900ft)	SEASON TO RUN	year-round	CHALLENGE LEVEL	beginner	WATCH OUT FOR	wet weather can cause mud

INVERIE & THE KNOYDART PENINSULA

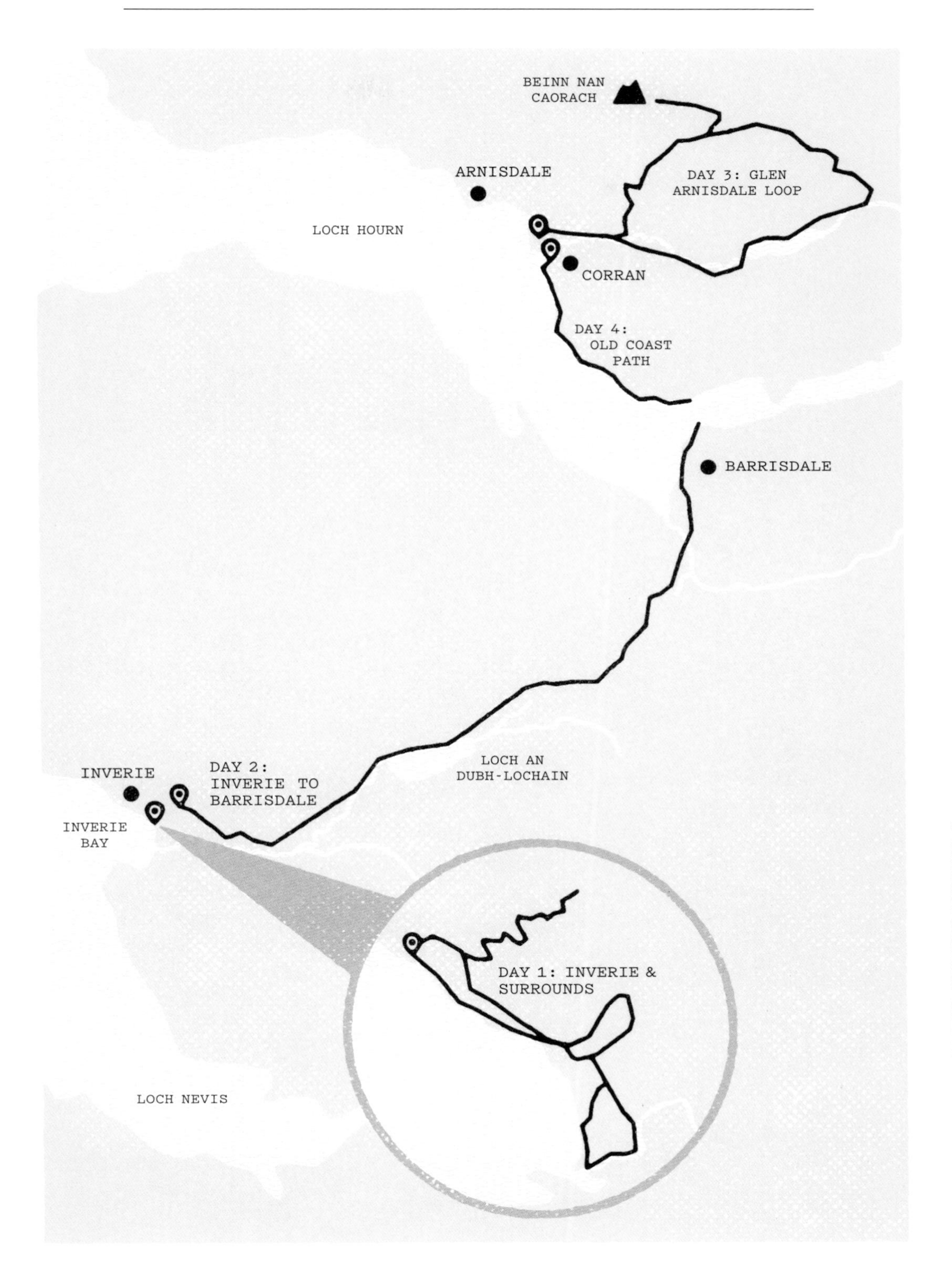

CORSICA
05
FRANCE: EUROPE

Corsica — France

ONE STEP AT A TIME

GUILLAUME PERETTI

Corsicans take time to appreciate their island's beauty – go a little way off the beaten track and you'll discover sparkling streams, white sands and welcoming local hospitality

Some people love France; others prefer Italy ... It could be said that Corsica is the lovechild of the two cultures. Lying south-east of the French mainland and west of the Italian peninsula, French Corsica is the archetypal island of contrasts. The epithet 'Île de Beauté' perfectly suits the fourth-largest island in the Mediterranean. Its 1,000km (620mi) of coastline comprises white, sandy beaches and rocky cliffs. Moving inland, you'll find hilly forests peppered with trails of soft pine needles, and gently sloping river valleys crossed by crystal-clear streams. And at Corsica's heart are rugged mountains, which make up two-thirds of the island.

Corsica is best enjoyed slowly, a step at a time – even when its spectacular running trails might call for a fast descent. Corsicans take time to appreciate their island's beauty, and don't like to be rushed. So take those extra steps and reach a more beautiful vantage point. Push on to the alternative hut just above the main trail to be rewarded with authentic Corsican hospitality.

A dense and well-marked network of trails – all part of the French Grande Randonnée (GR) system – criss-crosses the island north to south and east to west, with flavours to suit all appetites. The three Mare a Mare ('sea to sea') trails (Nord, Centre and Sud) take you from one beach to another, encompassing coastal and inland scenery and mid-altitude peaks. The two Mare e Monti ('sea and mountains') trails (Nord and Sud) lead from the comfort of the beaches to the central peaks. And then there's the mother of them all: the infamous GR20, a sixteen-leg north–south trail that follows the central spine of the island over about 180km (112mi) with around 12,500m (41,000ft) of elevation. Although it can be completed in one go (the current record, set in 2016 by François D'Haene, stands at 31 hours 6 minutes), the GR20 merits a slow exploration, taking time to appreciate the beauty of the landscape.

→ Running the cliffs of Pertusato, South Corsica.

For a three- to four-day trail adventure that balances classic Corsican highlights with lesser-known splendours, a good place to start is the town of Corte,

the historical and cultural capital of Corsica hidden in the island's depths. The route follows some of the Mare a Mare and GR20 legs, taking in a mix of medium and high mountains, before looping back past a stunning lake set amid the *pozzi* – areas of green pasture dotted with streams and pools only found above 1,800m (5,900ft).

Moving inland, you'll find hilly forests peppered with trails of soft pine needles, and gently sloping river valleys crossed by crystal-clear streams

The opening leg of this 77km (48mi) trail covers 22km (14mi), with 1,500m (4,900ft) elevation. Leave Corte along the Tavignano River: follow the Mare a Mare Nord orange markings up the gorge that cuts through the granite on a super-technical forest trail. The feeling underfoot will become familiar as you explore Corsica over the coming days. With its sparkling pools, the river offers numerous opportunities to refresh yourself, such as at the Russulinu footbridge. After the Sega refuge, the trail climbs another 5km (3mi) with 500m (1,640ft) of elevation before emerging out of the forest to bring you to your first destination: the Bergeries de Vaccaghja, one of which is manned by shepherd Noël, where you can stay the night and sample authentic Corsican hospitality.

The second leg is arduous and technical, covering 23km (14mi) with 1,000m (3,280ft) elevation – and it can easily be split into two days rather than one. Early in the morning, you'll discover Lac de Nino, nestled in another expanse of *pozzi*, an enchanting, supernaturally green high-altitude prairie. The GR20 markings northbound lead through a windswept, bare mineral world to the rather incongruous Hôtel Castel de Vergio, where you can stop for a coffee or lunch break. The trail continues relatively flat to the Bergeries de Radule (stop to check out the nearby waterfall), before a steeper section leads up to the Ciottulu di i Mori (Ciottoli) refuge, where you can opt to stay the night. If you do, and have an hour to spare before sunset, hike up to see the Capo Tafonato ('pierced head'), a geological formation just above the refuge, via a steep and exposed trail (with rope handrails in parts). The 55 x 16m (180 x 53ft) opening in the rocks – the largest natural arch in France – is the emblem of Monte Cinto, Corsica's highest mountain.

For a longer day, bypass the refuge and keep following the GR20 for another 7km (4⅓mi) and 400m (1,300ft) elevation via the charming Bergerie de Ballone

← The Asco Valley in the Cinto range; a view from the old Altore hut, which burned down during the 1990s.

→ Most of the Corsican Grande Randonnée (GR) trails are well marked in white and red signs or paint.

↓ The Bavella Range, which offers an Alpine feel with some technical passages.

↑ Sunrise on the Bavella
Range, crossed by the GR20
trail further south-east.

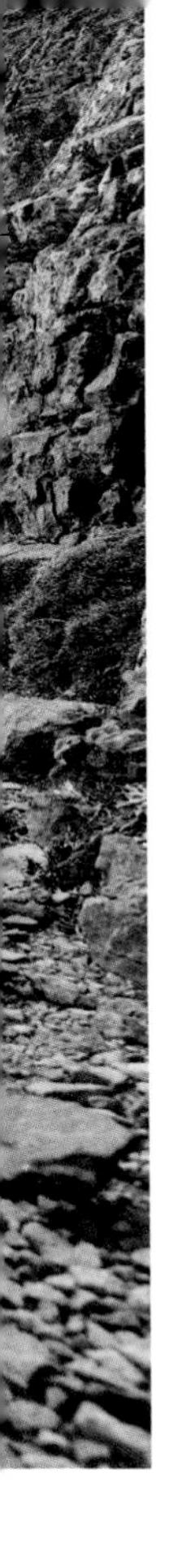

to reach the Tighjettu refuge. Perched at 1,683m (5,522ft) above sea level, the refuge is presided over by Charlie, one of the veteran wardens on the GR20 circuit and a jovial and charismatic host.

The following morning, set off for leg three (25.5km/15½ mi; 1,500m/4,900ft elevation) on the steep slope up along the crest towards the Pointe des Éboulis, where you can admire the profile of Monte Cinto. Monte Cinto, which at 2,706m (8,880ft) towers above the whole island, offers a breathtaking 360-degree panorama all the way to the sea. This is the highest point of this adventure, and from here you can savour the 15km (9mi) of downhill via the Refuge de l'Erco to the stunning Lac de Calacuccia. At Casa Vanella, in Casamaccioli, you can stop for the night (it's a proper B&B with all mod cons). The next day, you can take a taxi back to Corte, or add a picturesque loop back on foot.

I gave myself one year to prepare, and set my private life aside

The return to Corte could form an optional fourth leg of your adventure, 25km (15½mi) and 1,200m (3,900ft) elevation. A local trail brings you back to Corte along the crests, and past the famous Arch of Corte, a spectacular natural arch of weathered granite. From Casa Vanella, follow the valley up to Bocca di l'Arinella, then the crests to Bocca a Canaghia. You'll soon reach the Bergerie de Padule – one of the last water points on your way back – where you can buy cheese from the shepherd Michel Tucci. Just around the corner you will see the magnificent arch, before heading back down to Corte, retracing your steps along the high rocky paths, down through the forests and grasslands all the way to the town.

↑ A technical passage to reach the Capo Tafonato.

← Leaving the Réserve Biologique, a protected area of the Tavignano forest, to reach the mineral terrain above the tree line.

→ Take a small detour for a dip in the pool of the Cascade de Radule, just off the Mare a Mare route.

The GR20 has a long history of course records. In 2006, Pierrot Santucci had set a high bar of 36 hours 53 minutes. From the age of twenty, I dreamed of breaking that record. Then in 2009, Kilian Jornet achieved an incredibly fast FKT (Fastest Known Time) of 32 hours 54 minutes 24 seconds. His time shook me, but didn't deter me, and when I won my first ultra-trail race (the first edition of the 110km/68mi Restonica Trail, the first ever ultra-trail race in Corsica) in 2013, I thought that the GR20 record might be on the cards, given my intimate knowledge of the route. I gave myself one year to prepare, and set my private life aside. I launched my attempt in 2014, supported by a local team, and to my surprise set a new record of exactly 32 hours.

What I felt was indescribable. That record is my Olympic medal, the performance of my life. But it cost me dearly. The Corsican spirit was shaped by its mountain people, by the shepherds who share resources and stories, who lead a life close to nature, and let things happen in their own time. Forcing my own nature to achieve this record made me push too hard. I vividly remember the specific moment when my body and mind reached a 'point of no return' – where I knew that I should probably stop, or I would step through a door into uncharted territory.

As much as I was proud of this kind of Olympic medal of local trail running, I wasn't proud of having overdone it. The price to pay afterwards, mentally, was too high.

Now I always run in contemplation; I always make time and plan for the unexpected – and I encourage every runner to do the same.

→ (Opposite above): Trail runner Guillaume Peretti, near Lake Argento, just below Monte Cinto.

→ (Opposite below): Typical rockformations and trails of the Monte Cinto range.

↓ The *pozzi* (supernaturally green high-altitude prairie) of Lake Nino, encountered on day two of the trail.

GUILLAUME PERETTI

Guillaume Peretti works as a hydraulic dam technician in the mountains; his lunch break often involves going for a quick vertical kilometre to Monte Cinto above his workplace. From his childhood home in Cervione, nicknamed the 'Balcony on the Sea', on the sunny coast of eastern Corsica, Guillaume could glimpse the peaks of the interior, which always captured his imagination. And it was the summers spent at his grandfather's in Corte, central Corsica, that shaped his love for the island's rugged mountains: he moved to Corte when he was twenty-two. It came as a surprise to his outdoorsy, but not competitive, parents when at the age of just fifteen Guillaume asked to compete in the Via Romana, a 45km (28mi) race - he was so young that the organizers had to make an exception for him. He's been running ever since.

PRACTICAL INFORMATION

The island is easy to reach by plane, and also by land and overnight ferry from ports in mainland France and Italy. Initially set up for hikers, the Corsican trails are ideally suited to runners, with their short stages and dense network of huts, which allow for maximum flexibility. The official GR markings, in red and white, are clear and plentiful.

Following most guidebooks' advice to avoid the busy summer months, a lot of hikers now opt to take on the trails in June, early July or September – with the result that late July and August have actually become less popular.

Don't be fooled by the idea of an island: this is a land of mountains, with weather systems that can rapidly switch from T-shirt conditions to snow. Both June and September can bring thick fog and low temperatures, whereas August is the month of sometimes ferocious afternoon storms – while July promises the fewest surprises. Pack spare clothing accordingly.

You should aim always to carry 1.5l (around 3pt) of water with you, although the rivers and streams are generally safe to drink from.

Phone connection is usually good, although small pockets have no network coverage. All huts have a phone line and internet in case of emergency.

Accommodation is simple, and consists of refuges (set up for tourists, with a warden) and bergeries (shepherd's huts). While bergeries offer minimal comfort, and no showers, they will serve hearty meals and provide a bed or a tent.

Refuges all have cold (sometimes even hot) showers, and offer a single evening meal and a packed lunch, or a small shop. Pre-booking of a bed (or tent) through the National Park website is advised, but it is still possible to turn up without a reservation, especially at the bergeries that are not directly on the GR trails.

APPROX. DISTANCE	95km (59mi)	MAXIMUM ALTITUDE	2,706m (8,880ft)	CLIMATE	rapidly changeable; summer highs of 23°C (73°F)	TERRAIN	granite; pasture
APPROX. ELEVATION	5,500m (18,000ft)	SEASON TO RUN	June-Sept	CHALLENGE LEVEL	advanced	WATCH OUT FOR	steep ascents/ descents; limited water; unpredictable weather; residual snow

AROUND MONTE CINTO

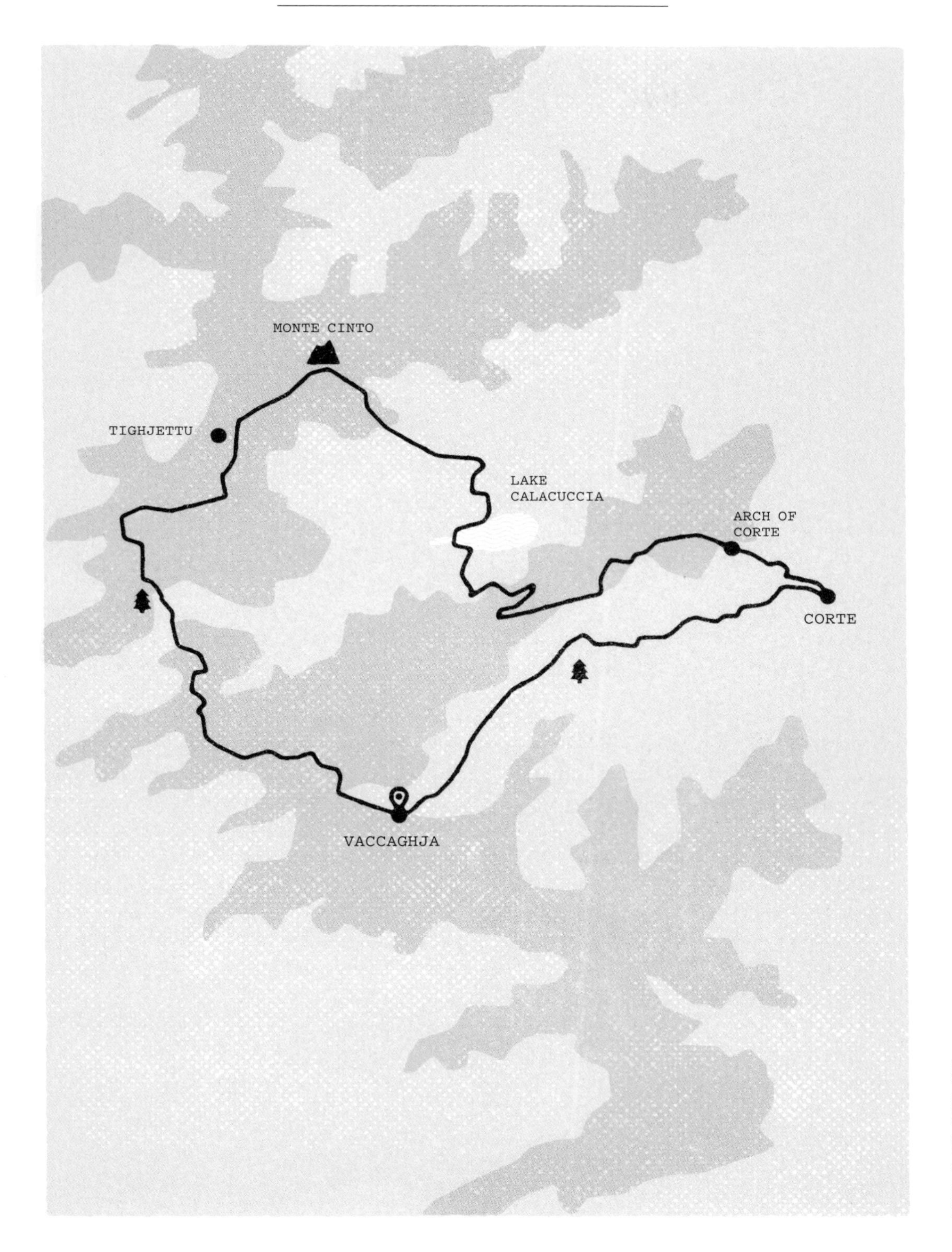

THE
PYRENEES
06
FRANCE/SPAIN: EUROPE

The Pyrenees — France/Spain

FINDING BEAUTY ON THE LOST MOUNTAIN

TOBIAS MEWS

The second-largest mountain range in Europe presents a unique mix of forgiving trails and steep climbs – and is relatively unexplored compared with the Alps

It's perhaps only when you open up a physical map of the Pyrenees that the entirety of the 435km (270mi)-long range can truly be appreciated. On the Atlantic side, the mountains of the Basque (Spain) and Pays Basque (France) are not especially high, but are rugged and untamed. These rolling hills offer some stunning trails and are host to the iconic Zegama-Aizkorri race, in the far western edge of the Spanish Basque country, and the Skyrhune race, in the French Pays Basque. Head inland into the central Pyrenees and the mountains get significantly steeper. The trails around the Ossau Valley, where the infamous Pic du Midi d'Ossau protrudes from the ground like a shark's fin among a scattering of mountain lakes, are nothing less than spectacular.

Although the second-largest mountain range in Europe, compared with the Alps the Pyrenees remain a wild and unexplored region. The French and Spanish Pyrenees are effectively two sides of the same coin, offering a pair of entirely different worlds to explore and run through.

On the French side, where the climate is mild and more humid, the mountains are all about steep climbs. Apart from the Corbières Massif, there are no real foothills to speak of. On the Iberian side, the foothills offer more forgiving trails. Nonetheless, the largest mountains are to be found in Spain, with Pico de Aneto claiming the highest spot (and also being the third-highest mountain in Spain).

Whichever side of the Pyrenees you are on, there are thousands of kilometres of waymarked trails to explore, more than half a dozen national and regional parks, six Stations de Trail® (designated and signposted trail-running centres), and much more. But with all except one of the valleys heading north to south, transport between each valley can be tricky.

← Rocky descent on the relatively unexplored Tour de Monte Perdido.

Without doubt, the two most famous trails, traversing the entire mountain range from the Mediterranean to the Atlantic, are the GR10 (France) and the GR11 (Spain). They are both challenging but offer different terrain and experiences. The more adventurous will be seduced by the Haute Randonnée Pyrénéenne (Pyrenean High Route), an unmarked but more direct trail that follows the mountainous spine of the range, criss-crossing the Spanish–French border.

The Tour de Monte Perdido (Lost Mountain) is arguably one of the greatest multi-day trails in Europe, though few people have heard of it. The name alone conjures up images of some sort of Lord of the Rings adventure. Factor in that this region of the Pyrenees is one of the least populated and least explored areas of Europe and it becomes even more alluring.

The trails around the Ossau Valley, where the infamous Pic du Midi d'Ossau protrudes from the ground like a shark's fin among a scattering of mountain lakes, are nothing less than spectacular

The Tour is just a few kilometres over a marathon – a 'meagre' 46km (28½mi). But the relatively short distance can be deceiving. With more than 4,200m (13,780ft) of elevation gain around the third-highest mountain in the Pyrenees (3,355m/11,000ft), passing through two countries, a UNESCO World Heritage Site and two national parks, it's by no means a walk in the park (no pun intended). Now add to the list the infamous Gavarnie Falls (among Europe's highest waterfalls), Roland's Gap (an incredible, toothlike gap in the mountain) and the Ordesa Canyon (the equivalent of the Grand Canyon in Europe), and trail runners get a lot of bang for their buck. Enchanting refuges (mountain huts) along the route on either side of the border make it possible to split the route into anything from two to five days.

Those lusting after more of a challenge could attempt the Tour de Monte Perdido Extrem – completing the trail in a single day.

↑ → Approaching Monte Perdido: a little bit of care and attention is required on this small section of via ferrata.

↑ Refuge des Espuguettes, with Roland's Gap in the distance.

There are two options for a starting point: Gavarnie, on the French side, or the official (and arguably the best) place to start, the beautiful Pineta Valley in the Aragonese Pyrenees, on the Spanish side. At the very end of the valley, tucked away near the banks of the Cinca River and surrounded by the steep sides of the mountains, is the Refugio de Pineta – the only refuge along the entire route that's accessible by car.

Those arriving for the evening meal will experience the impalpable air of excitement among their fellow guests, chatting about their day's adventure on the trails between hasty mouthfuls and gulps of red wine. Some are just passing through on their journey along the GR11, the 820km (510mi) route that spans the length of the Spanish Pyrenees. Others are planning a day's hike up to the Balcon de Pineta, with its panoramic views.

With a good night's sleep in the bag, an early start is vital if the circuit is to be completed in a day. The beam from the head-torch doesn't do justice to the scenery, as runners set off from Pineta, full of cheer and chat about the big day ahead. However, hidden behind the laughter are equal parts trepidation and excitement, as the GR11 zig-zags its way up a 1,300m (4,265ft) climb to the Balcon de Pineta. The rising sun casts an orange tint on to the limestone cliffs beneath and above you. Looking up, Monte Perdido stands proud.

Now is not the time to rest, however; it's just the warm-up. Passing a sapphire-blue lake, it's time to climb again, although now with hands and feet, before crossing an invisible line into France at the Brèche de Tuquerouye. Sandwiched

↑ Roland's Gap: compared with the Alps, the Pyrenees remain relatively wild and unexplored.

in the rock face is the highest refuge in the Pyrenees at 2,666m (8,747ft), and one of the oldest (inaugurated in 1890). Although not guarded, in the summer its twelve beds are regularly full.

The descent from the iconic refuge is treacherous with slippery scree and rocks aplenty, but not far ahead is the manned Refuge des Espuguettes, a notional checkpoint, if you will. It's also a welcome opportunity to grab a cold drink and some snacks while the resident donkey gazes at passers-by with a total lack of interest.

From the refuge, a smooth and flowing single track awaits you, a chance to let the legs loosen before the 'oh là là' moment. Indeed, it's impossible not to be overawed by the sight that awaits you. The French author Victor Hugo described it as: 'A mountain and a wall at the same time. It's the most mysterious building of the architects. It's the Colosseum of nature. It's the Gavarnie.'

The more adventurous will be seduced by the Haute Randonnée Pyrénéenne, an unmarked but more direct trail that follows the mountainous spine of the range, criss-crossing the Spanish/French border

The Cirque de Gavarnie is an enormous natural amphitheatre of limestone rock, with a 423m (1,388ft)-high waterfall tumbling down the cliff face. Here, you peel off the beaten path and scramble up a tricky and tiring section of rock known as the Échelle des Sarradets, using hands and feet to negotiate the loose

stones. High above you at 2,807m (9,209ft), what looks like a missing tooth in a child's smile is the Brèche de Roland – Roland's Gap. According to legend, the natural gap was made by Count Roland as he swung his magical sword, Durendal (France's version of Arthur's Excalibur), after being defeated at the Battle of Roncevaux.

To reach the hallowed Gap, it's necessary to cross the Glacier de la Brèche, which looks increasingly tired as the ancient ice succumbs to global warming. It's hard to take in the 40m (130ft)-wide and 100m (330ft)-high natural gap. Now would be a good time to do nothing but sit and admire the view and ponder its mysterious creation. But not for too long. There is little time to rest if you're going to complete the circuit in a day.

Luckily, the descent from the Gap, one that also marks the border into Spain, is smooth and easy – only interrupted by a small via ferrata section of trail, where care should be taken.

Once again, the landscape changes. There are no trees, just grass and layer upon layer of limestone rock. The constant climbing and descending takes its toll on the legs and the route between the Gap and the Refugio de Góriz can feel like an eternity. The refuge is an oasis of civilization in a moonlike landscape, and a welcome pitstop. It's tempting to feel slight envy at those settling in for the evening with a weary but satisfied look on their faces, some of whom are returning from summiting Monte Perdido.

It may be hard to tear oneself away from the refuge, but not far along the trail is a landscape that could have been lifted straight from a travel brochure in the USA. The similarities between the Ordesa Canyon and the Grand Canyon are easy to spot. Unshaped by man, it's a natural wonder of vast proportions. Far below, the Cascada de la Cola de Caballo tumbles down into the rift of the valley before joining up with the Arazas River. With superhero eyesight, it would be possible to see tourists making their way along the well-trodden path that follows the river to the waterfall. The scenery is simply breathtaking.

↓ The Ordesa Canyon, one of Europe's largest canyons.

The trail seems never-ending; it's easy to feel like giving up. But then the starting point appears in the Pineta Valley below. As the crow flies, you're not more than a few kilometres away from the refuge. But don't be deceived. There is still a way to go, especially on tired legs. What one imagines will take an hour will swiftly turn to two, as the reality of the painful 1,500m (4,900ft) of descent kicks in.

Yet as with every adventure, when the end is in sight you find the energy to push on, especially with the knowledge that dinner, served at 8.00pm promptly, awaits at the refuge. Locals and tourists alike casually walk along the river and glance up in your direction, greeting you with the customary 'Hola', unaware of the colossal journey you've just made. After all, most people take an average of four days to complete the Tour de Monte Perdido.

↓ Writer Tobias Mews running towards the Balcon de Pineta at sunrise.

When my wife and I decided that we'd move to the French Pyrenees, I spent hours – if not days – huddled over maps, tracing the valleys and their rivers, scanning for the high points and scrolling endlessly through Google Earth images showcasing the two sides of the Pyrenees, as contrasting as night and day.

It is hard not to be seduced by the humble splendour of the Pyrenees, whichever side of the coin you land. In a world where we are all connected by our telephones, as soon as you place your first step into the Pyrenees, you feel connected to something else: nature. As Victor Hugo wrote about his visit to the Pyrenees in July 1843: 'You may have visited the Alps, the Andes, the Cordillera, and now you have had the Pyrenees in front of you for a few weeks; whatever you may have seen, what you will see now is unlike anything you have encountered elsewhere.'

It is so true. The Pyrenees are a unique and unparalleled part of this planet. And a place that every trail runner should visit, even just once. And you never know, you may even want to move here.

↑ (Above left): The Gavarnie Falls, one of Europe's highest waterfalls.

↑ (Above right): Constant climbing and descending can take its toll on the legs.

TOBIAS MEWS

Tobias Mews is one of the UK's leading adventure journalists. He has tackled and written about many of the world's most iconic races, from the hot sands of the Marathon des Sables and the mountainous trails of the UTMB, to swimrunning among the archipelagos of Sweden's ÖtillÖ and fell running along the mountainous spine of Wales in the Dragon's Back Race.

Alongside his books *50 Races to Run Before You Die* and *Go! An Inspirational Guide to Getting Outside and Challenging Yourself*, his writing has appeared in many magazines and newspapers.

Although his journalism and pursuit of adventure have taken him around the world, the lure of the Pyrenees as a place to base himself and his family was too strong.

With his wife, Zayne, he now owns a bed-and-breakfast retreat for trail runners, cyclists and hikers called Secret Pyrenees, arguably the perfect base camp from which to explore the Pyrenees.

PRACTICAL INFORMATION

On the whole, the trails on the French side of the Pyrenees are far less 'runnable' than those on the Spanish, where groomed single track is more the order of the day.

The Tour de Monte Perdido (Extrem or multi-day) is not a route you'd ordinarily attempt on your own; phone coverage is patchy and the only way you leave the trail is by foot, stretcher or helicopter. Plus, much of the trail is above 2,000m (6,560ft) – even in June and July, when warmer weather opens up the passes, you're still advised to carry micro-spikes or crampons. Which basically leaves a four-week period between mid-August and mid-September for a fast, possibly snow-free attempt. Be aware that even in the height of the summer, it's possible to find patches of snow. And in August, book ahead for the Refugio de Pineta; it'll be busy.

APPROX. DISTANCE	46km (28½mi)	MAXIMUM ALTITUDE	2,815m (9,235ft)	CLIMATE	arid (Spanish side), humid (French side); summer highs of 27-30°C (81-86°F)	TERRAIN	rocky; grassy; scree
APPROX. ELEVATION	4,200m (13,780ft)	SEASON TO RUN	mid-Aug–mid-Sept	CHALLENGE LEVEL	expert	WATCH OUT FOR	patchy phone coverage; snow in summer; via ferrata climbing route

TOUR DE MONTE PERDIDO

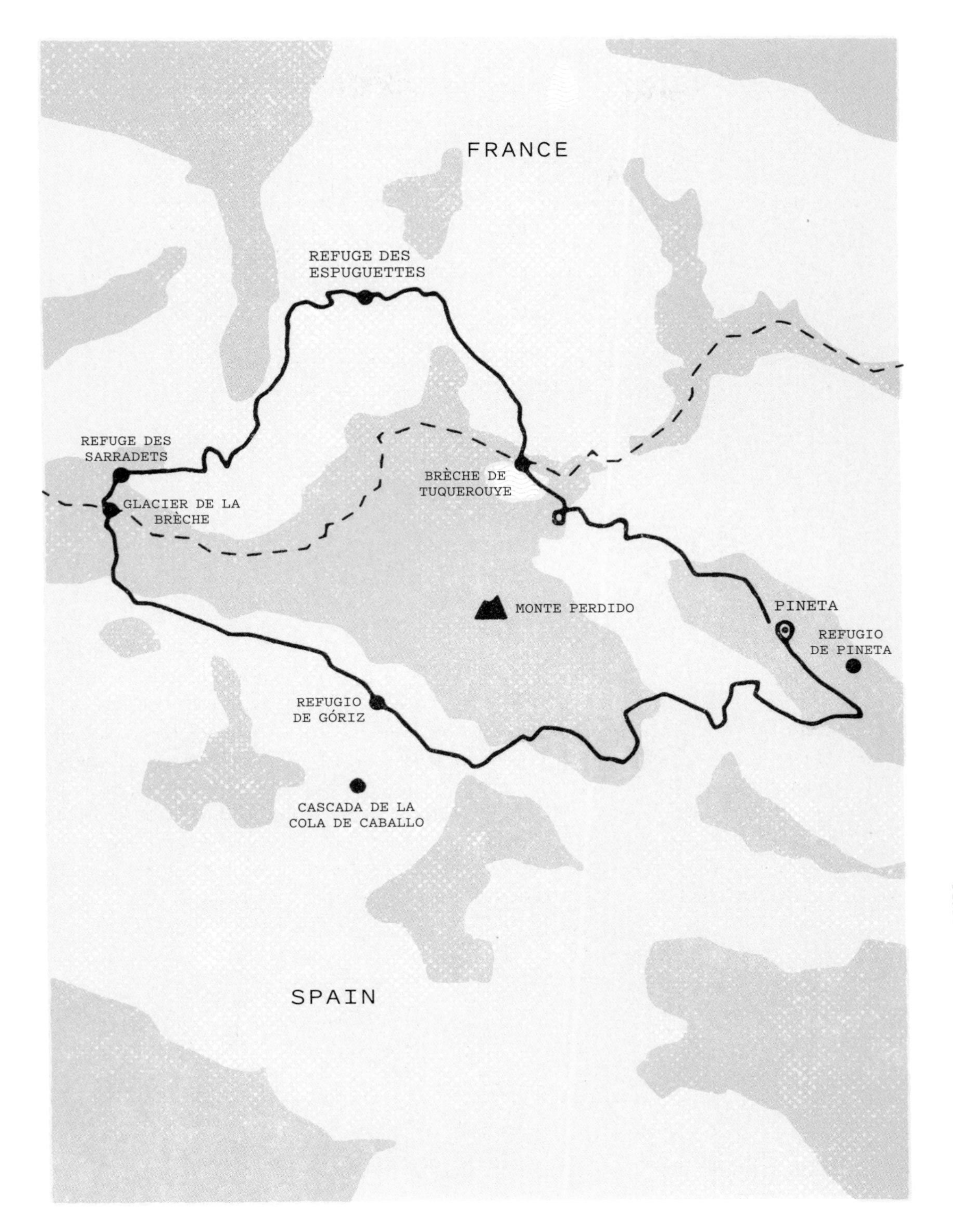

THE KUNGSLEDEN

07 | SWEDEN: EUROPE

The Kungsleden — Sweden

CARVING A PATH THROUGH THE SWEDISH WILDERNESS

ANNA GATTA

The Kungsleden weaves its way inside the Arctic Circle through some of Europe's most wild, bare and untamed landscapes, in a land moulded by extremes of weather

The Kungsleden – or Kings' Trail – is a 440km (270mi) artery that runs through the middle of one of Europe's largest nature reserves, connecting Hemavan in the south with Abisko, deep into the Arctic Circle, to the north. The trail was conceived by Svenska Turistföreningen – the Swedish tourist organization – at the start of the twentieth century as a way to access the wilderness on foot.

Along the length of the trail you'll find a range of Lapland environments, including birch forests at lower altitudes, wide open heathlands and rocky, bare alpine areas higher up, dotted with beautiful tarns and majestic peaks.

The most arresting views are to be found on the northernmost section of the trail, from Nikkaluokta via Singi to the end of the trail at Abisko. Most runners and hikers follow the trail north-south, but going in the opposite direction (finishing at Abisko) offers a couple of benefits: the opportunity to climb Sweden's highest mountain, Kebnekaise, before setting off on the run north; and the fact that you are heading towards the most beautiful part of the trail, which will be a treat to be savoured at the end.

One of the most important aspects of the Kungsleden is the environment through which it weaves. It is clearly in the extreme north and feels indisputably exotic. The trail carves its way through some of Europe's wildest landscapes, which are bare and untamed. The land appears to have been moulded by the climate, which in turn is driven by the Arctic winds. In a matter of minutes, the weather can change from blue skies and sunshine to windy and wet. That is all part of what makes the Kungsleden so special.

→ Multiple footbridges ensure that some legs of the route are truly runnable.

The trail passes through an area known as the Sápmi region – named after the indigenous Sámi people – which covers almost 20,000sq km (7,700sq mi).

An area around ten times larger than Luxembourg, it includes parts of Norway, Sweden, Finland and Russia. Yet there are fewer than 3,000 individuals living here, most of them Sámi people. Swedish Lapland forms part of this vast territory. The Sámi have inhabited this area for thousands of years, traditionally as reindeer-herders and fishermen. They are used to the cold that accompanies the winter months, but for many people who come to the region for the trails, the temperatures are a huge shock.

This part of northern Sweden contains the national parks of Stora Sjöfallet, Sarek, Padjelanta and the Abisko – spectacular areas full of glaciers and wild animals, including brown bears, lynx and reindeer. The stark beauty of this region is just one of the reasons it has been recognized by many outdoor enthusiasts as Europe's last remaining wilderness.

The trail is really well established and the hut system means that you can go fast-and-light

The Stora Sjöfallet National Park is dominated by the mountainous massif known as Áhkká, whose highest peak, Stortoppen (2,015m/6,610ft) is the eighth-highest in Sweden. From the top of the highest summit to the lake in the valley below is Sweden's highest vertical drop at 1,563m (5,128ft).

From Nikkaluokta, the easternmost extent of the Kungsleden trail, to its northernmost end at Abisko, is 105km (65mi), a section that can be covered in three or four days. One unusual aspect of the Kungsleden is its sections on wooden walkways, which keep you above the region's characteristically boggy ground and also help to prevent erosion. This means that the trail can accurately be described as runnable. So while most of the hikers stop for the night

at each refuge along the way, runners can leapfrog some of those stops – and even schedule an extra day to climb Kebnekaise.

One of the best things that anyone exploring this area can do is get off the beaten (or wooden) track. The right to roam is fiercely protected in Sweden – so even private land is open to the public. Along the trail there are many opportunities to take a detour and explore a lake or a valley. Or perhaps to climb a hill and see what the view is like.

Another quality of the Kungsleden is the lack of non-natural noise on the trail. When running or walking, visitors take in the views of mountains, lakes and forests in a kind of quiet meditation.

The start of the 105km (65mi) adventure is the refuge at Nikkaluokta, known as the gateway to the mountains. Start by following a narrow road from Nikkaluokta into the forest. The path soon becomes rockier as it passes the stunning Lake Ladtjojaure. The trail then continues uphill, crossing the Tarfalajakka River, and after 19km (12mi) reaches Kebnekaise Fjällstation (the mountain lodge at the foot of Kebnekaise). Keep an eye out for meditation spots. It's possible to take a boat across the lake, which takes 6km (3¾mi) off the overall length of the run.

Kebnekaise, with ten glaciers tumbling down its sides, rises to 2,015m (6,610ft) above sea level. If possible, set aside a day to climb the mountain: leave the refuge in the morning and return later in the day, staying the night before heading off along the trail again.

From Kebnekaise Fjällstation you descend gently 15km (9mi) to Singi. At this point you are above the treeline all the time, so the trail has the most Arctic feel

↑ These huts offer the chance to meet fellow runners and hikers, or just to rest tired legs.

← Huts managed by the Swedish Tourist Association (STF) are always well appointed and well managed.

↓ Just before Alesjaure, the peaks are bathed in rich red light.

→ There's always a warm welcome at the huts - and some offer unexpected comforts.

WÄLKOMMEN WELCOME
VAKKOTAVARE

VAKKOTAVARE
WASHINGPLACE
TVÄTTPLATS

↑ The reindeer is the emblematic animal of Lapland: expect to meet a few herds on the Kungsleden.

→ The Kungsleden carves its way through some of Europe's most arresting landscapes.

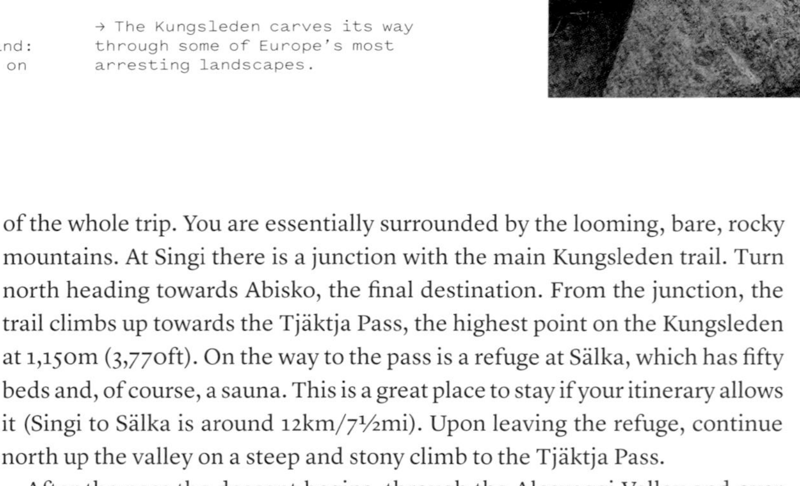

of the whole trip. You are essentially surrounded by the looming, bare, rocky mountains. At Singi there is a junction with the main Kungsleden trail. Turn north heading towards Abisko, the final destination. From the junction, the trail climbs up towards the Tjäktja Pass, the highest point on the Kungsleden at 1,150m (3,770ft). On the way to the pass is a refuge at Sälka, which has fifty beds and, of course, a sauna. This is a great place to stay if your itinerary allows it (Singi to Sälka is around 12km/7½mi). Upon leaving the refuge, continue north up the valley on a steep and stony climb to the Tjäktja Pass.

After the pass the descent begins, through the Alesvaggi Valley and over the Bossusjohka River. It's around 25km (15½mi) from Sälka via Tjätka to Alesjaure, and the Alesjaure refuge, perched on a hill, offers a fantastic view along the Kungsleden.

From Alesjaure to Abiskojaure is around 20km (12mi), over the now familiar terrain of bog, planks and the occasional rocky stretch. The refuge at Abiskojaure sits next to the wonderfully clear Lake Abisko, and there's a sandy beach that is perfect for those who fancy a dip – though be warned: the water can be bone-chillingly cold. Following the Abisko River to Abisko itself (15km/9mi), the trail crosses wetlands, ending up in the birch forest.

Along the Kungsleden, you may not encounter many indigenous people, but it is worth remembering that the Sámi use this land to raise their animals, especially reindeer. The herds are not considered dangerous, but it is advisable to be considerate of the animals, especially if there are young ones around.

The Stora Sjöfallet National Park is dominated by the mountainous massif known as Áhkká, whose highest peak, Stortoppen (2,015m/6,610ft) is the eighth-highest in Sweden

The other wildlife on the trails during the warmer parts of the year (from June to September) are mosquitoes (*mygg*) or midges (*knott*). Although mosquitoes are more common, the midges have a worse reputation.

Overall, the Kungsleden is a fantastic trail that allows you to experience an amazing part of northern Europe. The trail is well established and the hut system means that you can go fast-and-light. Just remember to take your time and explore as much of this magical place as possible.

↑ Huts are helpfully placed every 15-20km (9-12mi), meaning you can take the Kungsleden at your own pace.

↑ Wild nature and untamed landscapes are hallmarks of the Kungsleden.

→ Directions for runners and hikers are clear and simple.

When I lived in Sweden, I wasn't all that interested in exploring the nature there. In fact, I'd not been very far north of Stockholm. But what I saw when we arrived in Nikkaluokta really blew me away.

Growing up, I'd actually always had the feeling that Sweden was pretty flat. And indeed the southern part of the country, where most of the population lives, is made up of flat plains, some rolling hills and many huge lakes. But towards the sparsely populated north, there are definitely mountains. So despite the fact that the highest peak, Kebnekaise, is nowhere near as high as proper mountain ranges such as the Alps, the Himalayas or the Rockies – places I'd dedicated my life to exploring and where I tested my capabilities – I was delighted to find that there's plenty to keep the vertically minded interested. Truthfully, I was really not expecting what I found when I went to run a section of the Kungsleden, but the nature of the place is fascinating and pure.

↑ Runner Anna Gatta lives in Chamonix, but as a Swede she loved going back to her roots on the Kungsleden.

ANNA GATTA

Anna Gatta is a Swedish runner and climber with a great passion for adventure. She and her husband regularly spend weekends, and any other spare time, trail running or climbing for enjoyment and in preparation for their next adventure.

Anna has run extensively in France and many times in Nepal; she has completed the Atacama Desert Race, a 250km (155mi) rough-country foot race in Chile, and the Ultra-Trail Mount Fuji (84.7km/52½mi non-stop). One of her favourite runs is a twenty-five-day-long traverse from Slovenia back to her home in Chamonix, France, via the Via Alpina.

PRACTICAL INFORMATION

While the Kungsleden takes you through some of the most beautiful and wild parts of northern Europe, the trail itself is easy to follow and there is very little in the way of technical sections for which you need specialist equipment.

Climbing Kebnekaise isn't a significant challenge, at least not for someone with experience in the mountains. But it is worth remembering that you are a long way north, so there is always ice and snow on the peaks. It is possible to rent crampons at the Kebnekaise Fjällstation.

The weather can change fast, and when it does the conditions can be challenging. At the very least, waterproofs are essential – a good jacket and trousers that can be pulled on over your running kit. Waterproof gloves and socks are also worth considering. And if your pack itself won't keep your kit dry, then drybags would be a great idea.

If you use the huts along the route, then a change of dry clothes will make for a much more comfortable night. The same goes if you decide to camp, but even more so. Huts offer half-board, and it is also possible to buy something for lunch each morning before you leave.

It is possible to drink from the streams that you'll encounter along the way. But to be on the safe side, a water filter might be reassuring.

Finally, remember the midges and the mosquitoes. If you are tackling the trail when the temperatures are above freezing – generally the period from June to September – you are likely to encounter the flying nuisances. So take a net to wear over your head as you run.

APPROX. DISTANCE	105km (65mi)	MAXIMUM ALTITUDE	1,150m (3,770ft); Kebnekaise: 2,015m (6,610ft)	CLIMATE	Arctic: changeable	TERRAIN	heathland; boggy; rocky
APPROX. ELEVATION	3,200m (10,500ft)	SEASON TO RUN	June–Sept	CHALLENGE LEVEL	beginner	WATCH OUT FOR	midges; mosquitoes

THE KUNGSLEDEN

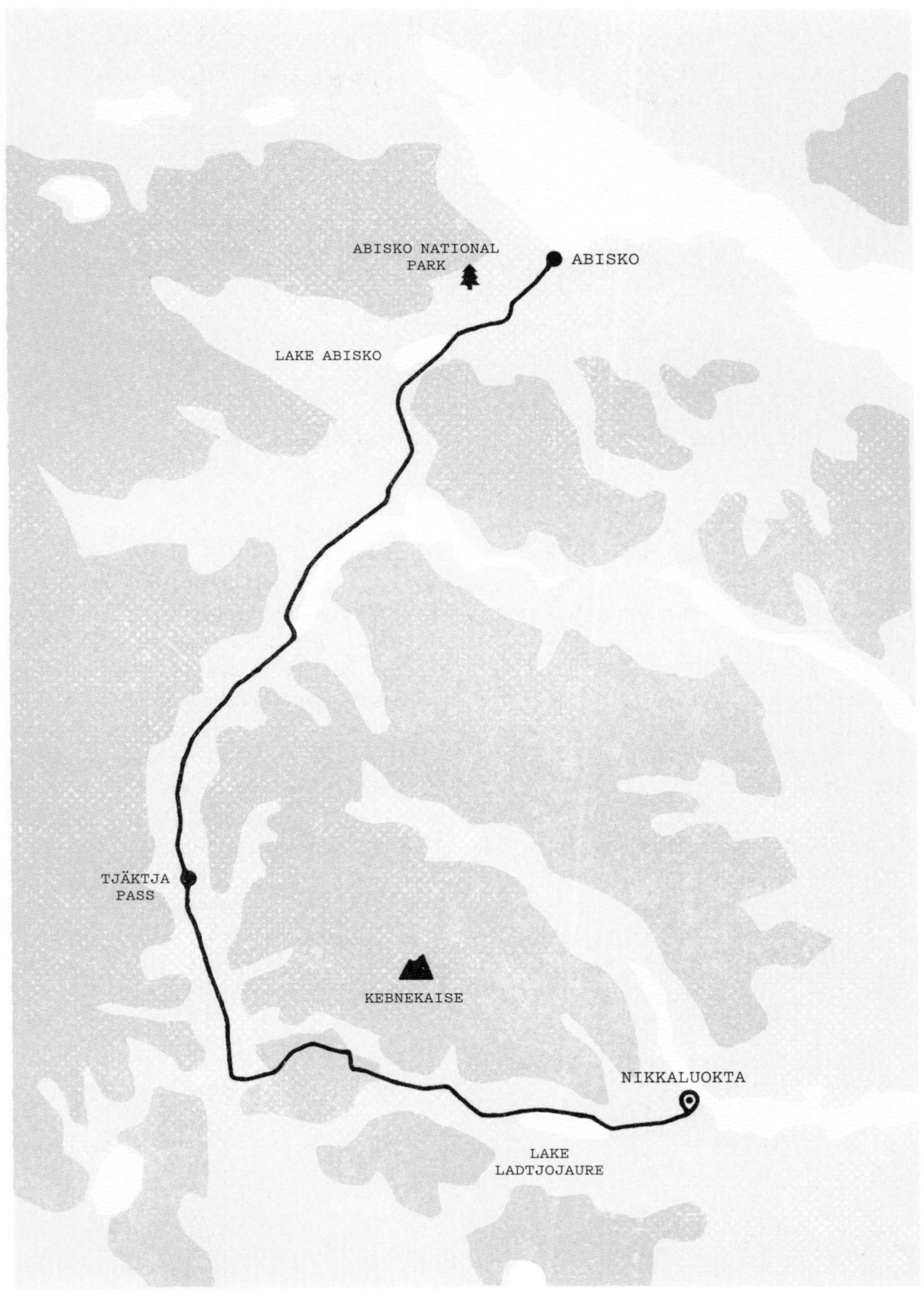

THE LAKE DISTRICT

08 | ENGLAND: EUROPE

THE LAKE DISTRICT — ENGLAND

The Lake District — England

LANDSCAPE & LANGUAGE YOU WON'T FIND ANYWHERE ELSE

RICKY LIGHTFOOT

Glacial mountain lakes and green valleys are the spectacular backdrop to some of England's most treasured trails

The English Lake District is a place where time seems to move more slowly, where field boundaries are marked by dry-stone walls and farmers work with their dogs to corral flocks of sheep. A place where even the dialect harks back to past times. From the moment you leave the main roads and start exploring the green valleys, long glacial lakes and craggy mountains, you are immersed in an area that feels rugged and steeped in history.

The Lake District is a national park nestled in the furthest north-west reaches of England, covering more than 2,500sq km (almost 1,000sq mi) miles and encompassing more than 200 fells – the name given to mountain peaks here. The breathtaking scenery is a consequence of the local geology: slate, limestone and sandstone formed over millions of years.

The way locals talk about running is deeply affected by the unique language of the Lake District. First and foremost, the sport here is called fell running. Organized fell races have taken place since the mid-1800s and they don't follow a trail – or even a prescribed route. Most fell races are low-key affairs where it is possible to sign up on the day, and many are short – not more than 10km (6mi). But there are also races and challenges of a much greater distance. The Bob Graham Round sees runners attempt to navigate and run between forty-two peaks, starting and finishing in Keswick, in less than twenty-four hours. This challenge was first set by guest-house owner Bob Graham in 1932; it involves around 106km (65 mi) of running and 8,200m (26,200ft) of ascent.

Keswick is a great place from which to explore the fells: the town of just over 5,000 inhabitants offers a wealth of places to stay or eat, and a good few pubs to enjoy a well-earned pint after a day outside.

← The last working slate mine in the UK near Honister, with the magnificent Haystacks framed in the distance.

One of the best ways to see the north-west Lake District is to run the route of the Buttermere Horseshoe – a popular, easy-to-follow walking route of around 23km (14mi). From Keswick, you can drive to the village of Buttermere or take the Honister Rambler bus.

From the Bridge Hotel, follow the road through the village towards the Fish Inn and take the bridleway to the left, which leads towards the shore of Buttermere itself. As you near the water's edge, you will cross Sour Milk Gill (gill is the Cumbrian word for a river or stream) and follow the path that crosses Burntness Wood, heading up to Bleaberry Tarn. From the tarn (small mountain lake), the route is steep and rough underfoot up to the summit of Red Pike, where you'll be greeted by breathtaking views into Ennerdale Valley. Beyond the head of the valley sits Scafell Pike, at 978m (3,209ft) the highest point in England, visible on a clear day.

From the top, wonderful views extend to Skiddaw and Langdale to the south, southern Scotland to the north and the Isle of Man off the coast to the west

From Red Pike, turn left, heading south-east towards High Stile. This is a rough place to be running and in bad weather is pretty exposed. From High Stile, the ridge continues to High Crag, then a short section of scree leads on to a manmade path through Scarth Gap and on up a steep climb to the summit of Haystacks. Here you'll find Innominate Tarn – known locally as 'no name tarn'.

The path down from Haystacks passes Innominate Tarn and Blackbeck Tarn, leading into an area that in the past saw a lot of mining activity. Heading north-east, you pass two relics of the mining age: Warnscale Bothy and Dubs Hut, built for eighteenth-century miners but now open to anyone who wants to spend the night (visit the Mountain Bothies Association website for more details). But be warned, they lack creature comforts.

↑ Author Ricky Lightfoot on the trail to Fleetwith Pike, with Buttermere coming into view.

← Warnscale Beck empties into Buttermere amid a contrast of bright grass and muted clouds.

From here the route takes you down to the car park at Honister Pass, where there is a youth hostel and a café. It's a good spot for a cup of tea to set you up for the next big climb to Dale Head. Follow the path leading away from Honister Pass alongside the fence heading north-west. The climb up to Dale Head is steep and grassy and sure to tax tired legs. At this point you are following part of the Bob Graham Round and the views from the impressive summit cairn are worth all the effort. A small path to the left follows the craggy edge towards Robinson and after a few hundred metres, a path to the right leads up to the summit of Hindscarth, well worth the detour. Descending Hindscarth, retake the path you were on, heading north towards Robinson, the last summit on the horseshoe.

To reach Robinson, follow the grassy fence line, around 200m (650ft) of climbing to the top. Descend via a steep path to the left, which is rough and rocky initially but then hits a grassy moorland plateau called High Snockrigg, where you can often see deer grazing. From here you simply follow the path back to Buttermere.

The second day's Lake District adventure follows a loop of around 19km (12mi) with 1,700m (5,600ft) of climbing, an extended version of a popular fell race called the Coledale Horseshoe, starting and finishing in the village of Braithwaite. Start in the car park at the foot of Whinlatter Pass and take the path up towards Grisedale Pike. This 3.2km (2mi) climb, pretty steep in places, involves three 'shelves' of flatter sections with steep climbs in between. Once you reach the third shelf, you will be greeted by the pyramid-shaped summit at 791m (2,595ft) above sea level, which explains why Grisedale Pike is known as the Lake District's Matterhorn.

↑ The breathtaking scenery is a result of local geology, formed over millions of years.

→ Buttermere is famed for its perfect glassy reflections.

↓ It's not all about the running; the Lake District is a place to pause and take in the views.

From the top, wonderful views extend to Skiddaw and Langdale to the south, southern Scotland to the north and the Isle of Man off the coast to the west.

From Grisedale Pike the path continues south-west towards Hopegill Head, a range of dark black peaks in the distance. Approaching the summit at Hopegill Head, Whinlatter Forest lies below to the north. The path here features a very steep drop to the right that is not for the faint-hearted. From the top of Hopegill Head, the route heads left towards Sandhill and then to the summit of Grassmoor, 852m (2,795ft) above sea level. Here you'll find a rough stone windbreak, a nice spot to take in the amazing views of three huge lakes visible from the summit: Loweswater to the north, Crummock Water in the middle and Buttermere to the south.

The breathtaking scenery is a consequence of the local geology: slate, limestone and sandstone formed over millions of years

A well-defined path leads to Crag Hill; then continue to the right of the cairn down a steep section known as the Scar on towards the next summit, Sail.

The descent from Sail features an elaborate set of fifteen switchbacks. The path takes you through a small pass and then up to the summit of Scar Crags, where a ridge path leads all the way to Causey Pike. Down from Causey Pike is an easy run to a four-wheel drive track that climbs up to Barrow, from where a simple 3.2km (2mi) run down a grassy slope leads back to Braithwaite – and the Royal Oak pub.

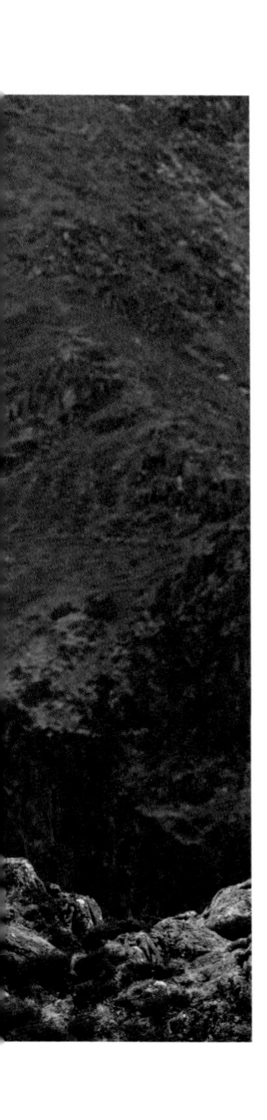

The third day in the Lake District starts at Swirls car park just south of Thirlmere village. The route itself is shaped like a lollipop, following a path up to Helvellyn, then a circuit around Striding Edge and finally retracing the route down from Helvellyn. The path begins by crossing a beck (stream) on a small wooden bridge, then follows Helvellyn Gill alongside Browncove Crags to the left. After a significant climb you'll arrive at the summit of Helvellyn at 950m (3,117ft).

Heading north-east, past the memorial to Charles Gough, a climber who fell to his death in 1805, the route follows Striding Edge, with Red Tarn below and to the left. The drop towards the tarn is notoriously steep; indeed, there are sections of Striding Edge where it is prudent to use hands as well as feet.

At the end of Striding Edge, the path becomes less treacherous. At the crossroads, take the route straight ahead up to Catstye Cam; the 200m (650ft) climb is worth the effort for the views down to Ullswater. From Catstye Cam, follow the path to the south-west on to Swirral Edge. This path is really rough, so take care. Follow Swirral Edge back to the summit of Helvellyn, where you'll reconnect with the path back down to Swirls car park.

← (Above left): Sunlight breaks through over Buttermere.

← (Left): On the trail towards Honister.

↑ Ricky enjoys a calm morning beside Buttermere en route to higher places.

What the runner will find following these routes is the extraordinary beauty and solitude contained in this part of the Lake District. This is where I feel most at home. Despite the chances I've had to race around the world as an elite trail and mountain runner, I'm always drawn back to the fells of the north-west Lake District because of their history, the physical challenge of running here and the opportunity to pick a line that has possibly never before been taken and head for a distant hilltop.

RICKY LIGHTFOOT

Ricky Lightfoot is a mountain athlete, born and raised in the Lake District and inspired to run by a teacher. As an international athlete, he has won numerous fell races, trail races and world championships. He works full-time as a firefighter and spends his free time - when he's not running - with his young family. Ricky will always call the Lake District home and remains fascinated by the history and characters that make this place so special.

PRACTICAL INFORMATION

The Lake District is one of the most popular outdoor tourist destinations in the United Kingdom. However, the roughness of the landscape and the severity of the weather should not be underestimated. It is claimed that 95 per cent of the visitors to the Lake District only venture 400m (1,300ft) from their cars – a statistic that should fill runners with joy because many fells will be almost empty. But this is also a reason to be cautious. Because of the remoteness of the Lakes, it is essential to always pack at least a waterproof jacket and trousers, a long-sleeved top and a foil blanket or lightweight bivvy (bivouac) bag (a waterproof outer cover that protects your sleeping bag and floor mat from the elements). You should also take a small first aid kit and make sure your phone is fully charged.

While you will find well-maintained paths and some signage, that is the exception and not the rule. Take a map and compass (that you know how to use), and make sure you pack enough water.

The Lake District has a proud tradition of hill farming, so be respectful of signs and instructions relating to livestock. And as always, leave no trace other than footprints.

APPROX. DISTANCE	52km (32mi)	MAXIMUM ALTITUDE	950m (3,117ft)	CLIMATE	Maritime: mild winters, cool summers (17-18°C /63-64°F)	TERRAIN	grassy; rocky
APPROX. ELEVATION	4,000m (13,000ft)	SEASON TO RUN	year-round	CHALLENGE LEVEL	advanced	WATCH OUT FOR	steep drops

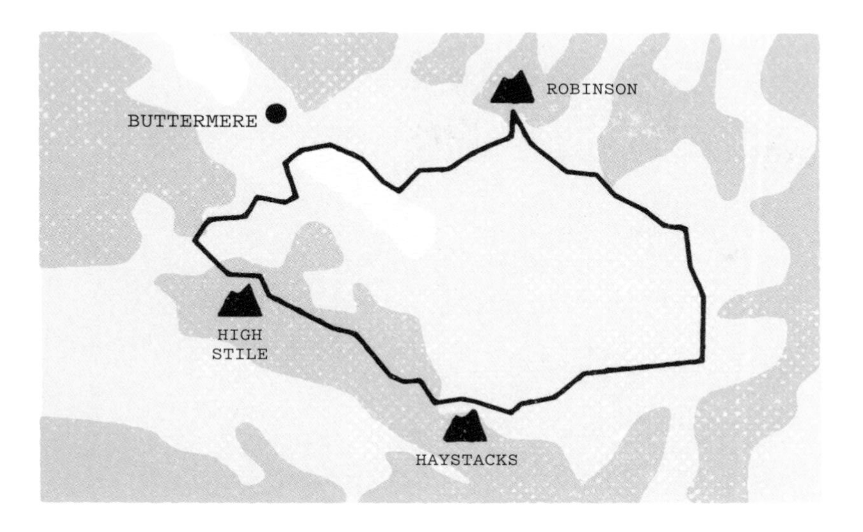

BUTTERMERE
HORSESHOE

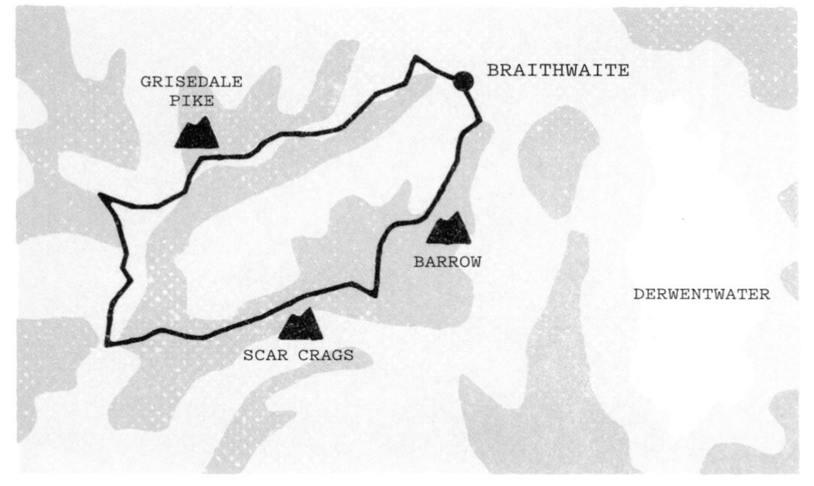

COLEDALE
HORSESHOE

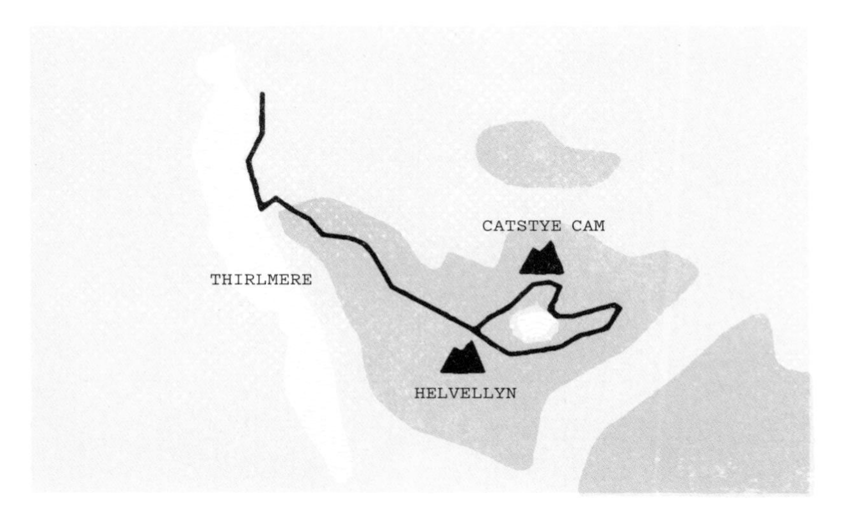

HELVELLYN

JURA

09 | SWITZERLAND: EUROPE

Jura — Switzerland

THE PERFECT INTRODUCTION TO THE SWISS TRAILS

JULIE FREEMAN

The Jura may not be as well known as the Alps, but the range is equally inviting: expect clean, crisp air, breathtaking views and seemingly endless trails

As the soft, single-track trails wind up the side of two modest forested hills, the noises of the once-mighty watchmaking industry gently trade places with subtle rural sounds: cows lowing, the occasional tractor, birds of prey crying as they float on the breeze, and the sigh of the wind in the pine trees. But mostly there is nothingness. Almost complete silence. In just forty-five minutes, the self-proclaimed 'watchmaking metropolis' of La Chaux-de-Fonds is replaced by the simple beauty of the Jura mountains. As you push up the hill, the bustle of the town fades into the background. This climb is perfect to get started: not too steep, not too technical, but enough to wake the legs up.

The modest Jura mountain range stretches over 300km (185mi) from Basel to Geneva and further into France, running parallel to the Alps, 100km (62mi) to the south. At its northern extent, the Doubs River acts as a border with France. At the southern end of the range lie the lakes of Biel and Neuchâtel, which sit 600m (1,970ft) below the crest of the Jura. But above the lakes, off in the distance, is the Jura's truly grandiose edge – an impossibly wide, uninterrupted view of the Jura's big sister range, the mighty Alps, with their imposing, ever-white snowy peaks.

← The Creux-du-Van in the foreground, with the Alps (and the mighty Mont Blanc) in the distance.

For many mountain enthusiasts, the Jura is all too easily overlooked – perhaps because of its proximity to the Alps and relatively modest profile. But this mountain chain should actually be seen as an ideal area for all levels of trail runner (unlike the Alps, which can occasionally represent too much of a challenge when the jagged peaks push towards the sky). The Jura is a slightly 'softer' place in so many respects. The people here seem to be easy-going; the trails are – in the main – easier underfoot than in many parts of the Alps; the weather is just a little less extreme. And yet there is still everything you need for a wonderful adventure: the air is clean and crisp, the views are breathtaking, the trails are seemingly endless.

Nestled at 1,000m (3,280ft) above sea level, on the Swiss side, the small town of La Chaux-de-Fonds is a perfect place to get used to the altitude. From here, countless one-day excursions are possible, from 10km (6mi) loops around town, to various viewpoints – for example, to the nearby Chasseral mountain – or further out by train to explore the high plateau of the Franches-Montagnes.

The Jura range provides an ideal playground for those who wish to get started in trail running in a forgiving environment. With a modest altitude (900–1,600m/3,000–5,200ft above sea level), permanent mobile phone signal, numerous food and drink options along the way, and plenty of accommodation every 10–15km (6–9mi), the main Chemin des Crêtes trail offers a perfect fastpacking adventure, which can be adapted to all levels of trail-running experience.

The Chemin des Crêtes, whose 320km (200mi) were signposted in 1905 all the way from Zürich to Geneva, is the oldest hiking trail in Switzerland. An excellent three-day route follows the trail for 90km (56mi) from La Chaux-de-Fonds to Vuiteboeuf. With a total elevation gain of 3,500m (11,500ft), it presents little technical difficulty, having only a few rocky sections and a couple

↓ Take time to appreciate the high cliffs of the Creux-du-Van on your way along the Crêtes du Jura.

→ A misty sunrise at the Creux-du-Van: keep an eye out for ibex.

of steep descents on single trails. Once you are on the crest, the trail is clearly visible. There's also the option to catch a train halfway.

The 90km (56mi) begins by heading on foot up towards La Corbatière, which is nestled in the wonderful Vallée de la Sagne, and sneaking between the towers of granite that make up Entre-Roche to find the tiny valley leading right, then left, up to Tête-de-Ran. In just an hour, your feet will have led you behind the mountain, and rounding the corner brings the reward of the first glimpse of a magical and unexpected panorama: the lakes at your feet, the Alps far beyond. A steep and short goat trail shoots up to the actual summit.

The trail alternates between a soft grassy feel and some rocky patches, so don't let the grandiose panorama trip you up

From Tête-de-Ran, following the ridge and keeping the Alps on the left would eventually lead to Geneva. But the next landmark on this particular adventure (and the trip's second-highest peak) is Mont Racine, at 1,439m (4,721ft). As the ascent begins, on the right you'll see France and its rolling hills, the blue line of the Vosges Forest, and even further the Black Forest in neighbouring Germany. On the left, the round top of Mont Blanc lies in the distance. The trail alternates between a soft grassy feel and some rocky patches, so don't

let the grandiose panorama trip you up. Mont Racine is a perfect spot to stop for a snack, because the amazing view disappears on the descent. Or stop for a leisurely lunch at La Grande Sagneule. There's accommodation here, too, if you want to cut the day short at 13km (8mi). Pushing on down the hill, it's another 4km (2½mi) to Montmollin or 13km (8mi) to Noiraigue, both options to spend your first night.

The second day begins by following the 5km (3mi)-long, steep single trail from Noiraigue, the 'Sentier des quatorze contours' (the 'fourteen-switchback trail'). When the trail flattens at the top and the trees suddenly stop, you'll be standing at the edge of a 150m (490ft) vertical drop, the rim of a natural amphitheatre-shaped cirque, which you can follow all along its 1,400m (4,600ft) walls to the other vertiginous side. This is the Creux-du-Van. The amazing Alpine panorama comes into view again here; it's a wonderful spot for lunch or even to stay the night at the Auberge du Soliat.

The modest Jura mountain range stretches over 300km (185mi) from Basel to Geneva and further into France, running parallel to the Alps, 100km (62mi) to the south

From the Creux-du-Van, after 20km (12mi) the ridge trail reaches Le Chasseron, at 1,607m (5,272ft) the highest point of the run. There are options for eating and sleeping here; alternatively, it's another 3.5km (2mi) down to Les Rasses, a tiny ski resort with charming chalet-style accommodation. Another option is a 5km (3mi) run via Le Cochet mountain, stopping at the Buvette des Avattes or the Buvette du Solier for a cold drink, down to Sainte-Croix, at 1,000m (3,280ft).

From Sainte-Croix, a 12km (7½mi) loop begins by going through the picturesque village of La Sagne up to a forest trail, through green pastures and back into the forest towards Les Aiguilles de Baulmes. Its rocky summit offers panoramas down to Lake Neuchâtel to the left, and Mont Blanc to the right. However, now it's time to turn your back on Mont Blanc and head north-east. After another hour of the toothlike ridge, the descent begins, through the forest back towards Sainte-Croix. From Sainte-Croix, you can either hop on a train or run down 4.5km (2¾mi) through the spectacular Covatannaz Gorges along the Arnon River to Vuiteboeuf, which marks the end of the 90km (56mi) adventure.

Running along the ridge also provides glimpses of a stunning lake. The train from Sainte-Croix back to La Chaux-de-Fonds goes via the medieval town of Yverdon, where you can stop and dip your toes in that same lake.

← With its undulating, non-technical trails, the Jura makes the perfect introduction to multi-day trail running.

↓ From the ridge, you can see lakes Neuchâtel, Bienne and Murten right at your feet, with Lake Geneva in the distance.

→ Pine forests offer some respite from the sun.

Having been born and raised in the foothills of the Jura, I didn't really understand the wonder of this overlooked section of mountains until I started trail running. Having graduated from road running in big cities to ultra-marathons in the steeper parts of the continent, I suddenly understood what I had not realized as a youngster – that the Jura is perfect for training and getting out into nature regularly, as well as racing. The mountain chain might not be as imposing as the Alps, but it is full of charm. Now I find myself happier than ever exploring the quiet trails that criss-cross the range, remembering some of my childhood outings in a very different light, through the eyes of a trail runner. And of course, the view of the Alps is incredible, so it always feels as though you are connected with the 'real' mountains.

↑ The view from Tête-de-Ran, the first summit you'll encounter, with the mighty Alps in the distance.

← Guide Julie Freeman making the most of the local trails, where hikers are few and far between, on a sunny May morning.

→ The view on the north side extends to France and Germany.

MEET THE GUIDE

JULIE FREEMAN

Born and raised in rural Switzerland, at the foot of the modest Jura mountain range, Julie Freeman thought she was the only trail runner in her family. However, she recently discovered that her maternal grandmother was a long-distance hiker. Julie unearthed a medal for the 50km (30mi) local race, which her nan completed three times while in her sixties. After fifteen years in London, Julie rediscovered her local mountains after moving back to her home country. Her favourite race is the Montagn'hard, a 68km (42mi) event near Chamonix that shares part of its course with the UTMB, with amazing aid-station buffets. Julie races for fun, not performance: mid-race, she famously waited for twenty minutes at the Miages aid station for the chicken and noodle soup to be ready. A former web developer, Julie is the co-founder and art director of *Like the Wind* magazine.

PRACTICAL INFORMATION

At this altitude, you may still find patches of snow until late April, so mid-May to early September are the best months to run this route. The trails will grow busier at weekends (especially in July), but don't expect large crowds.

In Switzerland, the footpaths are clearly marked with a yellow diamond-shaped sign, usually painted on a tree or stone. Yellow arrow signs will also indicate the destination – sometimes with an indication of the walking time.

This 90km (56mi) route offers plenty of flexibility: instead of taking three days, you could spend five days following the trails and taking in every view, or alternatively opt for a two-day, more intense training session (ideal early-season preparation for an Alpine race).

Auberges are a wonderful way to discover the trails on foot. They may not be luxurious, but this is more than compensated for by the warm welcome and the portion sizes. You can usually also buy a sandwich for the next day. Just be aware that the vegetarian and vegan options are often very limited, so it's worth planning or calling ahead. In most refuges, you can turn up bringing just a sleeping bag liner and will be provided with duvets or blankets. Some hosts might provide towels, but for the more rural locations it's prudent to pack a small microfibre towel. It makes sense to book accommodation in advance, so you can pay up front and enquire about showers, towels and sleeping bag liners.

Pack a long-sleeved top, a compact warm jacket, a waterproof jacket, a sleeping bag liner, a microfibre towel and lunch money in a small backpack, and leave your main bags in La Chaux-de-Fonds (the railway station offers large lockers for that purpose). La Chaux-de-Fonds is a train ride away from Basel or Geneva airports.

APPROX. DISTANCE	90km (56mi)	MAXIMUM ALTITUDE	1,607m (5,272ft)	CLIMATE	Alpine: 15-28°C (59-82°F) in summer	TERRAIN	soft; grass; rocky
APPROX. ELEVATION	4,000m (13,000ft)	SEASON TO RUN	May-Oct	CHALLENGE LEVEL	beginner	WATCH OUT FOR	snow; occasional steep descents

CHEMIN DES CRÊTES

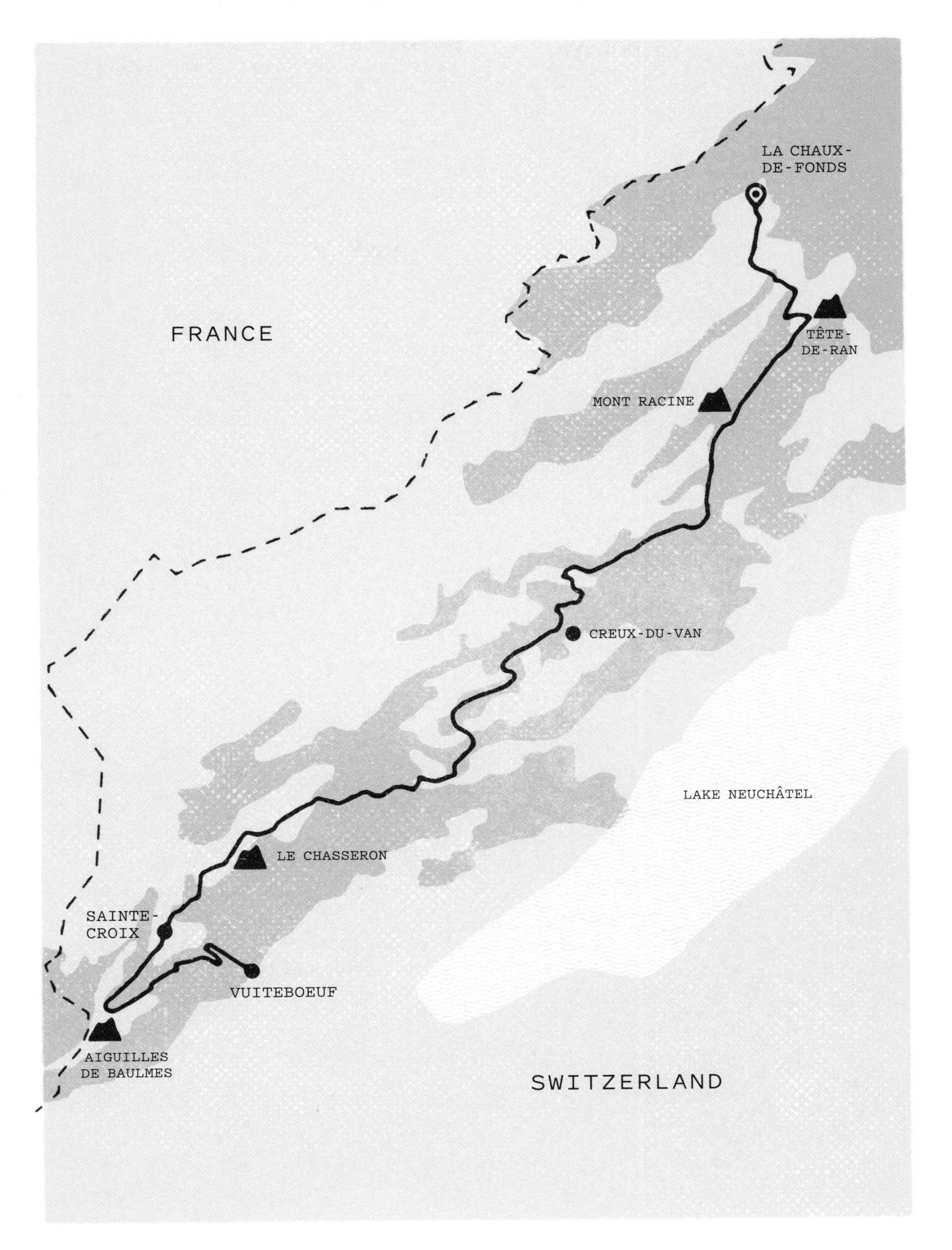

BRITISH COLUMBIA

10 | CANADA: NORTH AMERICA

British Columbia — Canada

UNLIMITED EXPLORATION FROM VANCOUVER

HILARY MATHESON

British Columbia is a huge, rugged world full of pristine, technical trails – not to mention some of the more colourful wildlife characters who call this vast wilderness their home

→ There are plenty of trails to follow, and it's rare that you'll come across another runner.

British Columbia, Canada, is a big place.

It's really big. Hailing from within the world's second-largest country, it almost can't help itself. For reference, BC easily dwarfs the entire United Kingdom – in fact, the UK could fit inside BC *forty times over* – while having a population thirteen times smaller than the UK. It has no shortage of trails to run and beautiful summits to seek out ... with rarely another soul to be found. Less than an hour from the modern cityscape of downtown Vancouver you'll find a wilderness laced with empty, technical trails and inhabited by a range of remarkable animals with whom we co-exist. Bears, bald eagles, bobcats and lynx might all be encountered during a run. It may seem daunting at first, especially when you consider the fact that you are far more likely to run into a bear than a human on the trails here, but this symbiotic relationship with the land and its inhabitants is also part of the allure.

British Columbia's very size commands attention, and being a trail runner in this wild country requires a level of self-sufficiency and preparation that shouldn't be underestimated. Trail running in BC may help you to become a more proficient mountain athlete, simply because of the variety of skills needed to conquer the technical terrain.

You do not have to venture far from civilization to have a proper adventure. Mount Seymour, part of the North Shore Mountains, is one of a trifecta of popular recreational mountains that creates an imposing backdrop behind North Vancouver. Mount Seymour is a short jaunt via public transport from the city, providing an instant escape from the concrete jungle and a go-to destination for panoramic sunsets cheekily shoehorned in at the end of a city workday.

Myriad mountain bike trails meander up the mountain for a 'choose your own adventure' route, but if views are what you're going for, then it pays to

↑ Time your run to coincide with sunrise or sunset at the top and you'll be rewarded with tremendous views.

head for the top. The winter resort parking lot also serves as the trailhead for summer trail lovers, and from there all (non-motorized) roads lead uphill. As you pass underneath hibernating chairlifts and over slopes covered in summer wildflowers, there are choices to be made. Either take the long way around several hidden mountain lakes, their pretty reflections of the treed landscapes imbuing them with gentle Pacific Northwest beauty; or, if you are fighting daylight and chasing sunset, make straight for the top. Vistas abound from the three summit peaks, and on a clear day views extend all the way to Mount Baker in Washington, USA. Bugs and bears proliferate on the hillsides in the summer, so it's still important to pack proper backcountry gear, even for destinations close to the city. The most accessible adventures still require a healthy dose of respect and preparation for the wild country that we cohabit.

For a slightly bigger day out, a trip to Squamish is a must. The drive along the Sea-to-Sky Highway from Vancouver – arguably one of the most beautiful highways in the world – leads to the 'Outdoor Recreation Capital of Canada'. There are certainly no shortages of turquoise, glacier-fed lakes to be found in Squamish, one of the most beautiful being Watersprite Lake. The trailhead is accessed via a forest service road requiring a four-wheel drive vehicle, and the trail then meanders pleasantly through boulder fields and scenic meadows.

Look out west as you gradually climb and you'll be treated to stunning views of the Howe Sound, which flanks Squamish. After a short but punchy pitch of steep, root-filled terrain, a shimmering, turquoise-coloured lake reveals itself, presided over by the imposing tower that is Watersprite Mountain. The lake's otherworldly colour comes from the glacial silt swirling throughout the icy water, reflecting the sunlight. This 18km (11mi) out-and-back route is best enjoyed during mid- to late summer, when the alpine flowers are still blooming and the hillsides are covered in wild blueberry bushes.

As you pass underneath hibernating chairlifts and over slopes covered in summer wildflowers, there are choices to be made

As far as access to the alpine goes, we really do like to earn our views in BC. Most Alpine destinations require at least a few hours of uphill zig-zagging along steep tree-lined trails in order to gain the ridgelines. There are some hidden gems that allow for slightly faster Alpine access (providing a higher ratio of 'bang for buck') – notably Needle Peak, which is situated along the Coquihalla Highway, approximately two hours east of Vancouver. However, don't be fooled by the relatively short 13km (8mi) return distance. This challenging route climbs steeply upwards from the trailhead, launching you into the distinctive ecology of the subalpine in less than an hour.

The terrain changes quickly as you climb; from the distinctive lush forests for which Canada is known, the scenery morphs into a layer of scrubby and hearty subalpine foliage that seems impervious to the harsh winds and weather that often pummel the landscape. Finally, the trail tops out above tree level, revealing

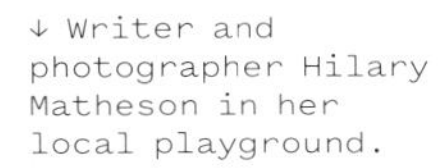

↓ Writer and photographer Hilary Matheson in her local playground.

↑ Watersprite Lake's amazing colour comes from glacial silt reflecting the sunlight.

panoramic views of the entire mountain range. From here, in the cradle of a natural saddle, the options are endless. You can explore the beautiful alpine granite and neighbouring vantage points that surround Needle Peak, take a swim in one of the clear alpine lakes that beckon tired travellers, or scramble up to the top of the steeper summit (a fairly straightforward climb featuring a few short sections of spicy exposure, with some route-finding via oft-camouflaged cairns). When perched on the dramatic and often windy peak, on a clear day you get a spectacular view of the entire mountain range as it extends across the border and into the US portion of the Cascade Mountains. Anyone making the trek up to Needle Peak in May or June will find there's still enough snow for some fun glissading down the slopes on the descent.

For a longer adventure, the West Coast Trail is probably the best-known point-to-point route in BC. Located within the Pacific Rim National Park on Vancouver Island off the coast of Vancouver, its 75km (46mi) length is often tackled as a five-to-seven-day backpacking trip, but it can also be completed as a fastpacking trip over a few days. The trail features many beautiful beach campsites, as well as unique terrain including cable-car crossings, suspension bridges and many, many ladders. Lush and pristine, this area is home to a wide variety of wildlife and marine life.

On an even bigger scale, the Sunshine Coast Trail, at 180km (112mi) long, is Canada's longest connected hut-to-hut trail – and a daunting, but equally rewarding, beast to tackle. Its mossy, vibrant, single-track paths feature stunning old-growth coastal forests, waterfalls, views of the Salish Sea, and picturesque huts that are free to use and operate on a first come, first served basis.

→ (Opposite above): Small wooden huts are rare sights in the open BC landscape.

→ (Opposite below): The distinctive lush forests of Canada, on the way up to Needle Peak.

↓ Some of the trails require some serious scrambling.

↑ A mid-run viewpoint, looking out at the vast expanse of the North Shore Mountains.

I have lived in British Columbia my entire life, and I still feel as though I've explored only a small fraction of this province, even though as an ultra-runner and professional outdoor photographer I have spent countless hours criss-crossing this massive province's mountain ranges. I've raced up to the top of Mount Seymour and back down to sea level as part of the aptly named 'Bucking Hell' ultra-race; I learned to backcountry ski on its family-owned winter ski resort. Some of my most memorable fastpacking experiences (and some of the worst chafing of my life) have happened along the gruelling Sunshine Coast Trail.

Having travelled all over the world for work and play, I still find myself blown away by the untouched grandeur of this land I am proud to call home, and my desire to see more of it only grows increasingly insatiable with each new area I explore. Living in a place as vast as BC, with all its unspoiled and untouched playgrounds, there are just two questions I regularly ask myself. One: how much time can I devote to appreciating more of this beautiful land? And two (most importantly): how much chocolate and cheese am I going to need to eat to fuel all of those adventures?

↑ Running through the Cascade Mountains, where summer weather frequently collides with the last vestiges of winter.

↓ Mount Seymour is a short jaunt from Vancouver, providing an instant escape from the concrete jungle.

HILARY MATHESON

Hilary Matheson is an award-winning outdoor photographer, graphic designer and videographer based on the Sunshine Coast, BC. She is a competitive ultra-runner and mountain athlete, and her endurance training allows her to cover large distances in remote corners of the world while hauling around heavy cameras and gear.

Hilary grew up on a small farm in BC and has always had an appreciation for a life lived outdoors - but as her passion for the mountains has grown, so too has her love for the beautiful country she calls home.

While her adventures and projects have taken her all over the world, she has also realized that it's not just incredible places that move us and inspire us - it's the people in those places: people, and their very human journeys to which we can all relate. She seeks to distil and communicate their stories, struggles and triumphs visually through her work.

PRACTICAL INFORMATION

With very little mobile phone coverage outside urban areas, it is essential to pack enough gear in case you have to spend the night outdoors in an emergency. An inopportune ankle sprain could turn the simplest trail run into an overnight trip.

As trail runners' skills progress and they venture further and higher into the backcountry, many also start to develop other complementary skillsets, such as glacier travel or abseiling, in order to help them go further afield. Overnight trips also bring their own wildlife challenges. You may find yourself packing bear spray as habitually as water filters, debating the merits of carrying bear canisters with you for safe food storage, or getting creative with stashing your food at the top of nearby trees to discourage any nighttime visitors. If you stop to sample those delicious blueberries, consume in moderation and make sure you're practising good bear etiquette. If you don't scare the bears, chances are very good they won't scare you. Nothing worth having comes easily, but it is always worth the work.

This isn't designed to scare you off – most visitors will never have a negative animal interaction, and most misadventures in the backcountry are a direct result of poor packing or bad weather, which are universal challenges. But in order to appreciate the scale of adventure in BC in particular, one must appreciate the scale of the place, and respect it accordingly.

It should also be noted that the amount of gear needed for these routes increases exponentially once the trips get longer, as there is little opportunity to reach civilization mid-adventure for a resupply. And as you climb higher (for example, Needle Peak), mountain weather can change rapidly. Even on a bluebird day it's worth packing emergency gear for potential snowy squalls.

APPROX. DISTANCE	106km (65mi)	MAXIMUM ALTITUDE	2,095m (6,873ft)	CLIMATE	changeable – even in summer temperatures can dip to single figures	TERRAIN	forest; foliage; meadow; rocky
APPROX. ELEVATION	3,500m (11,500ft)	SEASON TO RUN	May-Sept	CHALLENGE LEVEL	expert	WATCH OUT FOR	patchy/no phone coverage; changeable weather; bears; residual snow

NEEDLE PEAK TRAIL

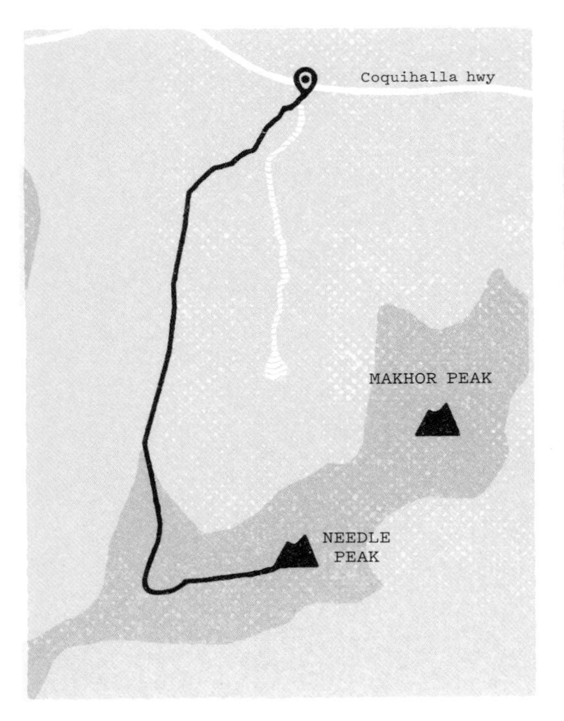

WATERSPRITE LAKE

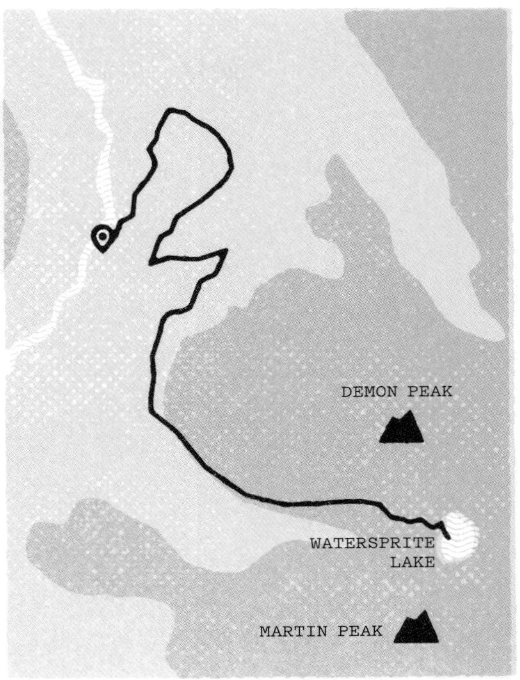

WEST COAST TRAIL

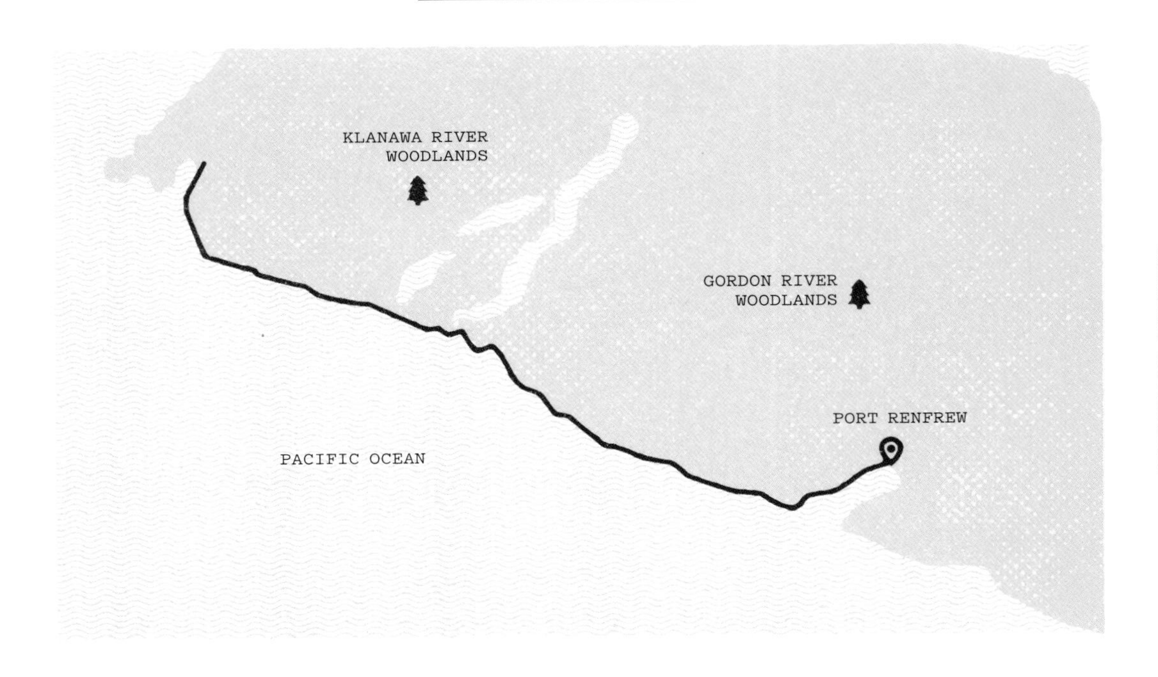

THE WHITE MOUNTAINS

11 | USA: NORTH AMERICA

The White Mountains — USA

PICTURESQUE PRESIDENTIALS & PEMI

STEFANIE BISHOP

Surrounded by names evoking American history, the trails of the Pemigewasset and the Presidential Range are technically challenging, and enhanced by the amazing views

The White Mountains may lack altitude on paper, but the peaks stand tall from the valleys below. More than 2,000km (1,240mi) of marked trails through multiple ecozones reach summits with views as far as 210km (130mi) on a clear day. There is no shortage of physically demanding terrain: switchbacks are rare and steep trails over rocks and roots commonly require runners to engage their full body. The notoriously harsh weather can increase the difficulty of even mild trails, especially in winter. Though it may feel strenuous, all it takes is one quintessential White Mountain summit in this ever-evolving landscape to vitalize your soul and lure you in for more.

The White Mountains are in New Hampshire, about 320km (200mi) south of Montreal, Canada, and are mostly public land, specifically the White Mountain National Forest, state parks and federal land. These mountains inspired some of Robert Frost's poetry; for a few years, his front porch gazed upon the Franconia Range.

The Lincoln Woods Trailhead, just outside Lincoln, marks the start of a grand adventure. It's the gateway to the Pemigewasset Wilderness and the start/finish of the 'Pemi Loop'. A suspension bridge crosses a wide section of the Pemigewasset River; it's worth taking a moment here. The Lincoln Woods Trail, once the location of the Lincoln Railroad, is wide and gentle, with a grand tunnel-like feeling created by a canopy of tall trees. The Pemi River roars off to the right. During peak foliage you'll be immersed in a brilliance of warm colours. This area is as accessible as it is picturesque, with routes of all distances and difficulties. Once you turn off the main path on to the Osseo Trail, you'll drift away from the crowds and into the forest.

→ Ascending Mount Lincoln from Little Haystack along the Franconia Ridge.

↑ Immersed in the astounding allure of the Franconia Ridge Trail, with Mount Flume off in the background.

→ Running north on the Crawford Path from Mount Monroe and Lake of the Clouds Hut.

It's a gentle, short warm-up run to the Osseo Trail, continuing along a charming brook. A distinct right hairpin turn signals the belly of the climb up to Mount Flume, the shortest peak of the Franconia Range at 1,319m (4,328ft). It's steep, tightly carved into the forest, featuring large rocky steps, roots and wooden ladders. The Mount Flume summit is narrow and rocky, with alpine evergreens. Extensive views showcase the valleys and far-off peaks.

The descent from Mount Flume is typical of the region: rocks of all sizes, exposed roots, and the occasional need to hold on to a tree for extra support.

Continue on the Franconia Ridge Trail until reaching the summit of Mount Liberty, whose grand diagonal slabs pierce the sky. It offers runners unobstructed views towards the rest of the Franconia Ridge.

Shortly after leaving Mount Liberty, under the cover of trees, the Franconia Ridge Trail merges with the Appalachian Trail (AT). There's a nice rhythm to the Franconia Ridge, beginning at Little Haystack Mountain (where you emerge from the trees to an exquisite, unobstructed panoramic view), over to Mount Lincoln, and lastly to Mount Lafayette at 1,603m (5,260ft). The runnable ridgeline invites you to open up and let your legs go, but also makes you want to take your time – although, when the weather turns, it is as brutal as it is beautiful.

Mount Lafayette is undoubtedly the pinnacle of the immediate region. Even on days when the ridge is completely submerged in cloud, it's generally easy to navigate. Be cautious, though: mountain weather changes quickly.

Leaving Mount Lafayette, the Garfield Ridge Trail continues 5.6km (3½mi) towards the final peak of the Franconia Range, Mount Garfield. After running down the last slabs of Mount Lafayette, you'll weave through mossy hardwood and evergreen forests, passing Garfield Pond before making a shaded ascent to the summit.

These mountains inspired some of Robert Frost's poetry; for a few years, his front porch gazed upon the Franconia Range

Continuing on the Garfield Ridge Trail towards the Galehead Hut, the trails are quintessentially north-eastern, manoeuvring down steep, uneven, rocky terrain through the trees. Following a good rain, the trail after the Garfield Ridge Campsite turns into a miniature waterfall.

The Galehead Hut, one of eight Appalachian Mountain Club (AMC) huts in the White Mountains, feels like a friend's cabin deep in the wilderness. It's just off the main trail and is a great place to relax or spend the night.

Galehead Mountain, part of the Twin Range, is a short climb from the hut, with its only views from an outlook shy of the summit. Not everybody climbs Galehead; some prefer the spectacular views of South Twin Mountain.

The Twinway Trail leads up a short, punchy climb to South Twin Mountain. Chunky rocks stand like giant breadcrumbs, over a near-350m (1,150ft) climb in about 1.2km (¾mi). Evergreens flank the trail, unveiling the summit and the surrounding landscape.

↑ Morning clouds rising
from the valley below
Mount Liberty.

The trail becomes gentler, lined with alpine bushes and trees. Crossing a small boulder field, continue on to Zealand Mountain or run the Bondcliff Trail for a worthwhile 8km (5mi) out-and-back of Mount Bond and Bondcliff (which completes the main peaks of the Pemi Loop). Mount Bond is a pleasant run: moderate terrain, covered in low flora and with a clear view, but the showstopper is Bondcliff. True to its name, the vast summit stops abruptly as an incredible cliff drops down towards the middle of the Pemi Loop.

Back on the Twinway Trail, towards Zealand Mountain, you pass over Mount Guyot. The Zealand summit is treed-in but the views from Zeacliff, a short side trail further down the Twinway, make up for it. Zealand Falls, next to the Zealand Falls Hut, is a delightful waterfall that cascades over layers of rocks.

Consider a run up through the boulder field to Mount Washington for sunset, especially if you don't plan to summit it at sunrise or in the morning light

You'll connect with the A–Z (Avalon to Zealand) Trail, passing Zealand Pond. The ascent from Zealand Pond to the col leading to Mount Tom snakes through hardwood forests. There's a short climb to the Mount Tom junction, and then the trail leads to your final descent to the Highland Center, a perfect place to rest for the night before the Presidential Range, a route of approximately 32km (20mi).

There are many options when tackling the Presidentials, including the direction, and adding peaks not on the 'official' traverse route. Though it has greater vertical gain, the north–south route is the more popular; some find the south–north route a greater psychological challenge because of the taller peaks in the latter half.

However, one advantage of travelling south–north is the magnetizing energy of Mount Washington constantly in view once you exit the treeline. Starting your traverse across from the Highland Center on the Crawford Path, a moderate trail climbs about 5km (3mi) to the Mount Pierce junction.

Mount Pierce is a short out-and-back detour off the Crawford Path on the Webster Jackson Trail, marked by a large cairn and surrounded by evergreens.

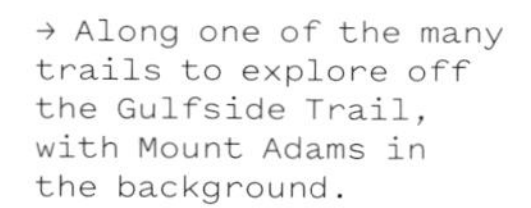

→ Along one of the many trails to explore off the Gulfside Trail, with Mount Adams in the background.

On a clear day you can see the southern peaks of the Presidential Range. Continuing on the Crawford Path (again linked to the Appalachian Trail) to Mount Eisenhower passes through thick shrubbery and alpine grasses and flowers, eventually exposing you to these mountains' notoriously vicious weather.

The trails are clearly marked; you'll spot hikers and possibly other runners. Mount Eisenhower and Mount Monroe are accessed via trails that split off the Crawford Path, known as their respective 'loops'.

The Lakes of the Clouds lie in the col beneath Mount Monroe and Mount Washington, the tallest mountain in the north-east at 1916.5m (6,288ft). You'll find the highest AMC hut here – in front of it, delicate flowers and vegetation fill the landscape between large boulders around a mountain lake.

There are a few options from the hut, all rewarding in their own way. If you're not staying at the hut, a quicker, yet still scenic way out (approximately 8km/5mi) continues to the summit of Mount Washington then drops down via the Tuckerman's Ravine Trail towards the AMC Pinkham Notch Center. Getting down Tucks is technical, but afterwards it's easier and scenic.

Consider a run up through the boulder field to Mount Washington for sunset, especially if you don't plan to summit it at sunrise or in the morning light. At 1,917m (6,289ft), Mount Washington is the highest point in the north-east. Inside the large visitor centre is the Mount Washington Observatory, a museum and a snack bar. Visitors can access the summit via the Auto Road or the Cog Railway. It can get overcrowded during weekends and holidays, but by staying

↓ Reaching your first White Mountain summit will vitalize the soul and make you hungry for more.

at the Lakes of the Clouds Hut you'll have the flexibility to summit during quieter hours.

From the hut, it's about 17.7km (11mi) to the northern end of the traverse, running over Mount Washington, picking up the Gulfside Trail, as well as the 'loops' of Mount Clay and Mount Jefferson. The trail continues along rocky yet verdant terrain, even passing an enticing grassy field between Mount Clay and Mount Jefferson called the Monticello Lawn.

Breaking off at the Thunderstorm Junction, the penultimate peak, Mount Adams, offers a clear view down to Star Lake, the Madison Spring Hut and Mount Madison, your final summit. There are a few routes down Mount Adams, the eastern route shorter but steeper; keep in mind the wind before making a decision. The trail up Mount Madison from the hut leads up a rocky spine to the final cairn.

While the Valley Way Trail is the 'official' route of the Presidential Traverse, the Air Line Trail is more scenic. Reconnect with the Valley Way further down by the Snyder Brook and its multiple small waterfalls to the Appalachian Trailhead. If you spot a place along the brook where you want to soak your legs, now is the time – it's a relaxing way to complete your journey through this iconic region of the north-east.

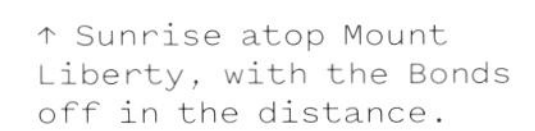

↑ Sunrise atop Mount Liberty, with the Bonds off in the distance.

← There is no shortage of physically demanding terrain.

→ Lowe's Path off Mount Adams; large cairns help lead the way.

↑ Picking away at the Gulfside Trail, the alpine flora dusted in frost.

→ Choosing your route is straightforward on these well-marked trails.

→ (Opposite): The White Mountains have been a training ground for runners for more than a century.

Even though I live just outside New York City, I consider these majestic mountains an extension of my home. I've emerged from the trails in the summer after a long, hard run, feet sore, covered in mud and sweat, thinking about a local beer; and in the winter, wearing every layer in my pack, returning to my truck by headlamp, my only concern turning on the heat. As many hours as I've spent in the White Mountains, I still feel like I've only covered a small percentage of the region. Even while I was filming a passion project on the Pemi Loop over the course of half a year, every familiar place we recorded always had a sense of a freshness.

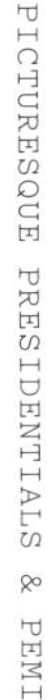

STEFANIE BISHOP

Stefanie Bishop is a multi-sport endurance athlete and champion obstacle course and adventure racer, as well as a private coach and interior designer, based in a suburb of New York City. She specializes in multi-day races, finding that she thrives on the challenge of sleep deprivation and the unknown that accompanies it. She is a lifelong New Yorker and though she lives an hour from the nearest mountain, her 'no mountain, no problem' approach to training has enabled her to navigate them confidently and successfully. She continually dreams up and maps out ambitious adventures.

Stefanie is an advocate of all sports, especially trail running and mountain biking, having found that her own experiences have translated into finding success in everyday life, and she inspires others to do the same. Her life mantra continually motivates her to push above and beyond her limits and, most importantly, appreciate the adventure.

PRACTICAL INFORMATION

The White Mountains have some of the harshest weather on Earth, especially high winds. Even if the Mount Washington Observatory Higher Summits Forecast looks optimal, bring adequate layers to stay warm, rain gear, and an emergency/first aid kit. It may get cold up high, even in August. And don't forget bug spray. If the weather report deems it too dangerous to travel above the treeline, there are alternative runs from Lincoln Woods, the Highland Center and Pinkham Notch.

The best time for this adventure is June–September, when the AMC huts are open, offering meals and snacks. Book overnight stays in advance via the AMC website. Camping is popular, but read the rules: campfires are prohibited, and there's no camping in the Alpine Zone where trees are shorter than 2.4m (8ft), within 60m (200ft) of trails and waterways, and within 400m (¼mi) of a hut or an official campsite. The formal backcountry campsites are fee-based and have outhouses and usually a nearby water source. These are filled on a first come, first served basis. Store your food in bear-proof containers.

There is no on-trail water source after the first climb until the Garfield campsite spring. The huts have spouts; check with the AMC that they are open. Treat water from natural sources appropriately.

This running adventure relies on public transport: the Concord Coach from Boston, Massachusetts, to Lincoln, and from Pinkham Notch back to Boston (reservations required). If you are not driving, get a taxi from Lincoln to the Lincoln Woods Trailhead. By car, park at the Highland Center and take the AMC bus to Lincoln.

It's not uncommon for runners to complete the Presidential Traverse and the complete Pemi Loop in a day, but back-to-back is ambitious given the terrain. To get the most out of your experience, take your time.

APPROX. DISTANCE	66km (41mi)	MAXIMUM ALTITUDE	1916.5m (6,288ft)	CLIMATE	Continental sub-Arctic	TERRAIN	rocks; roots; ridges; forest
APPROX. ELEVATION	5,300m (17,500ft)	SEASON TO RUN	June-Sept	CHALLENGE LEVEL	mixed	WATCH OUT FOR	wooden ladders; harsh winds; limited water in some places; bears and moose

THE WHITE MOUNTAINS

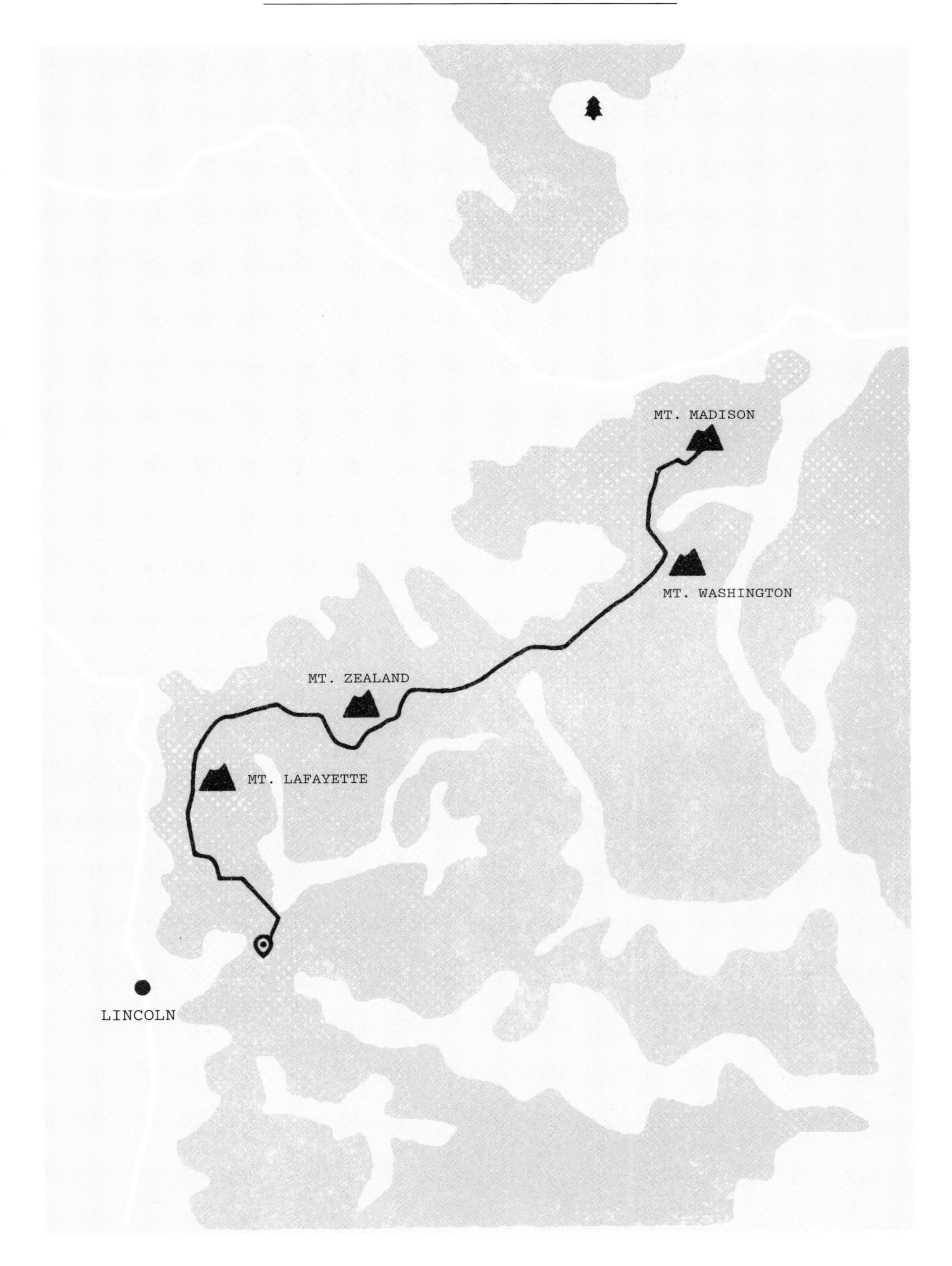

HOTEL
MONTE VISTA

SEDONA & FLAGSTAFF

12 | USA: NORTH AMERICA

Sedona & Flagstaff — USA

JUST LIKE THE MOVIES

ROB KRAR

The red and orange rocks of Sedona are familiar from photographs and films, and their majesty highlights the power of time and nature

Approaching Flagstaff, your eyes are drawn to the large mountains that dominate the skyline. Sacred to thirteen tribes in the region, this unique geographic feature – covered by snow during the winter months – is the remains of an ancient stratovolcano.

These mountains are the San Francisco Peaks; locals call them simply 'the Peaks'. The crowning glory is the highest point in Arizona, the 3,850m (12,633ft) Humphreys Peak. Trails and dirt roads are abundant on the San Francisco Peaks and all around the mountains' base, weaving through open meadows, stately ponderosa pines and quaking aspen trees. The diversity of flora and geology in the area is astounding. The mountains of Flagstaff, the red rocks of Sedona, and the descent into the Grand Canyon all highlight the awe-inspiring power of time and nature.

When most people think of Arizona, they picture arid desert, saguaro cacti and lonely, barren landscapes. Visitors are often surprised to find an oasis of trees, and to learn that the ski resort has an average snowfall exceeding 250cm (100in). Nestled at the base of the mountain lies Flagstaff, a casual and friendly city full of river-rafters, runners, hikers, skiers, climbers and bikers.

There's a special place in the heart of the city for running, and the sport has a long, deep and meaningful history in the region, being a rich tradition in many indigenous cultures.

The 15km (9mi) Hangover Loop in Sedona is a route originally created by mountain bikers looking for a thrill, and it's also not uncommon to see climbers on the spires towering above. Energy builds during the beautiful drive to the

← The Arizona canyons are technical, arduous and best suited to experienced trail runners.

↑ ↓ With its proximity to the Grand Canyon, Sedona and the San Francisco Peaks, Flagstaff has become a mecca for trail and road runners.

→ The area's varied landscape might often look familiar from old-time Western movies.

trailhead. Halfway through the 45-minute drive from Flagstaff, the two-lane highway suddenly opens up from the pines and drops into Oak Creek Canyon. Peaks of red rocks begin to emerge, offering striking views of the formations you are about to run on and around.

The trail begins by winding through scrubby desert and dry washes, crossing the dirt road a few times. As it begins to climb higher, the view opens up and you are on the rock that makes Sedona so photogenic. The famous red and orange sandstone has graced the cover of just about every outdoor magazine. These sand dunes and deposits from an ancient inland sea continue to be shaped by wind and water into fantastical shapes. It's the kind of landscape familiar from an old-time Western movie – in fact, this area was used heavily in film-making during the late 1940s and 1950s.

An improbable path follows the cliff line with steep drop-offs on one side and, at times, a wave of cliff curling overhead on the other

Take in the view on the way to the high point, a small pass on the formation above. Drop down the other side and run the traverse that gives this loop its name: an improbable path follows the cliff line with steep drop-offs on one side and, at times, a wave of cliff curling overhead on the other. Views are abundant as the trail winds back down to the return path to the parking lot.

The 30km (18½mi) Peaks Loop is a local favourite, connecting three of the best trails in Flagstaff. It starts slowly: a rocky first section (1.6km/1mi) begins the traverse along Kachina Trail east to the Weatherford Trail. Rolling up and down for 8km (5mi), the trail passes through stands of aspen, open meadows with views of Flagstaff below and quiet pine corridors to the intersection with the Weatherford Trail. This wide trail began its life in the 1920s as a proposed toll road on which Model T Fords would ferry tourists to the highest point in Arizona.

The incline is often runnable, with ever-expanding views as you climb up through pine, spruce and aspen, past open patches of seasonal wildflowers. Finally, the last long switchbacks climb above the treeline, crossing several avalanche paths and offering views down into the inner basin and out into the painted desert, before reaching a high point at 3,650m (11,975ft) on the shoulder of Agassiz Peak.

The 1,000m (3,280ft) descent begins here. Less than 1.6km (1mi) later, at Humphreys Saddle, there's an option to take on a rugged, technical 3.1km (2mi) side trip out and back to the summit of Humphreys Peak. Descending the switchbacks to the ski area, this technical trail is the most popular in the area. Bomb down, or take it easy and soak up the quiet forest, intermittent views and glimpses of other large avalanche paths. Pop out of the trees and the wilderness area and across the bottom of the ski resort to complete the loop back to the car.

Many visitors to the Grand Canyon take at least a partial walk on the Bright Angel and South Kaibab trails starting from the South Rim. These trails hug both sides of the Colorado River at the base of the canyon – the other trails to do so are the North and South Bass trails.

↓ Around Sedona (here near the Hangover Loop), the inclines are often runnable.

→ (Opposite above): Arizona is not all desert and canyons: author Rob Krar in the meadows on the A-Z Trail near Snowbowl.

→ (Opposite below): On the Kaibab Trail, steep switchbacks descend through distinct rock layers representing four million years of geological history.

HOKA

↑ Rob Krar near the SP Crater,
a cinder cone volcano.

↑ Rob Krar on the Bass Trail during their ‘rim-to-rim-to-rim’ crossing in 2020.

→ A section of the 15km (9mi) Hangover Loop in Sedona.

→ (Opposite): Supermoon in Arizona.

While bridges allow for safe travel across the river at Bright Angel and South Kaibab, the Bass Trail is open water and only for those experienced with fast-moving rivers. For our route, the river will be your turn-around point; you'll gain a taste of the epic views and unique silence of the Grand Canyon by running a 24km (15mi) out-and-back on the South Bass Trail – a run that begins with a 960m (3,150ft) descent that you will have to earn back on the return.

The adventure starts with an early wake-up call to drive 116km (72mi) to Tusayan, where a 45km (28mi) dirt road leads to the trailhead. In the primitive parking area you will see remnants of the tourist venture of the trail's namesake, William Bass. During the late nineteenth and early twentieth century, this was the main tourist access to the Grand Canyon. Bass expanded the existing trail system to take guests to the river, where at one time a cable system ferried them across to the north bank.

The route was nearly 70km (43mi) and included swimming across the Colorado River in our birthday suits

The run begins on steep switchbacks descending through distinct rock layers representing four million years of geological history. There's a short reprieve as the trail crosses the flat Esplanade plateau of beautiful red rock, before it sharply descends the red wall into Bass Canyon itself. The rest of the run traverses in and out of the dry canyon bed, descending to the impressive Bass Rapid on the mighty Colorado River. Spot the old boat chained to a rock – it was abandoned in 1915. The beach is a nice spot for a break, and maybe a quick dip in the river. Return the way you came, admiring the impressive cliffs as you climb back out. Keep an eye out for condors and bighorn sheep.

↑ Running in the San Francisco volcanic field, 40km (25mi) north of Flagstaff.

The trails of Flagstaff and the surrounding region truly are a special place for me. Without the community and landscape I would not be the athlete or person I am today. I often wonder where my life would be if in 2005 I hadn't 'temporarily' moved here. On the trails and in nature, I found a renewed strength and love of running, and a sense of peace and grounding to guide me through difficult times. Trail running has allowed me to open up about my struggle with depression, to share, and to help others with their own issues.

The Bass Trail had been on my bucket list for some time. But when my friend Mike Foote texted in December 2020 asking me if I was interested in attempting a challenging route within Grand Canyon National Park, I declined, feeling I lacked the necessary fitness and motivation. However, I just couldn't get the invite out of my mind, and on the final day of the year I found myself staring across the Grand Canyon. The route was nearly 70km (43mi) and included swimming across the Colorado River in our birthday suits. The remoteness, cold temperatures and grey skies made the run all the more challenging and intimidating. We finished in 11 hours 32 minutes, exhausted: this effort undoubtedly ranks among my greatest and most fond memories of my athletic career.

↑ The Peaks Loop, looking back down to the north side from the saddle between the sacred San Francisco Peaks.

↓ The Peaks Loop, looking east towards the inner basin between Agassiz Peak and Humphreys Peak.

ROB KRAR

Rob Krar grew up canoeing and cross-country skiing in Hamilton, Canada, where he gained an appreciation for nature, conservation and land management. Although he ran competitively during high school and university in the USA on a scholarship, his relationship with running ebbed and flowed until he found his true calling on the trails, mountains and wilderness in 2009.

Achievements include twice winning both the Western States 100-Mile Endurance Run and the Leadville Race Across the Sky 100-Mile race; twice being voted North American Ultra-Runner of the Year; and being named one of the '50 Most Influential People in Running' in 2015.

Rob speaks openly about mental health, sharing his struggles with depression to raise awareness and reduce stigma, especially in the endurance community. He uses his trail running success to advocate for the protection of public lands, and shares his knowledge through mentoring, coaching and hosting running retreats in Flagstaff.

PRACTICAL INFORMATION

The Peaks Loop begins at Arizona Snowbowl ski resort; park at the base and follow the signs to the Kachina Trail. An early start is important in the summer months to avoid being caught in possible monsoon thunderstorms later in the day and allows time to enjoy this challenging and technical loop.

The Bass Trail requires experience and careful planning. In order to attempt a 'rim-to-rim-to-rim' run across the canyon and back, you'll need to be highly skilled at swimming, open water and/or rafting skills. We therefore suggest an out-and-back 24km (15mi) route, turning back at the river.

The South Bass is easily the most remote trail on the South Rim. Getting there is half the adventure and requires a four-wheel drive vehicle with good clearance, confident driving skills and careful planning. Another great option is to obtain a camping permit from the Park Service to spend a night car-camping right on the rim before or after the run (or both). The reward for the journey is a day with the Grand Canyon largely to yourself. The trail is easy to follow with a map. There are no signs, but cairns at the junctions with trails to Royal Arch and the almost 160km (100mi) Tonto Trail.

An important consideration for running in Sedona and the Grand Canyon is the extreme temperatures during the summer months, often exceeding 40°C (104°F). Begin hydrating early and drink often, and don't be surprised if you consume double the amount you initially planned for.

APPROX. DISTANCE	74km (46mi)	MAXIMUM ALTITUDE	3,650m (11,975ft)	CLIMATE	extremely hot summers (up to 40°C/104°F) and possible monsoon thunderstorms	TERRAIN	rocky
APPROX. ELEVATION	15km (9mi) to 30km (18½ mi)	SEASON TO RUN	Apr-Nov	CHALLENGE LEVEL	advanced	WATCH OUT FOR	stay hydrated during summer; no signposts on South Bass Trail

PEAKS LOOP

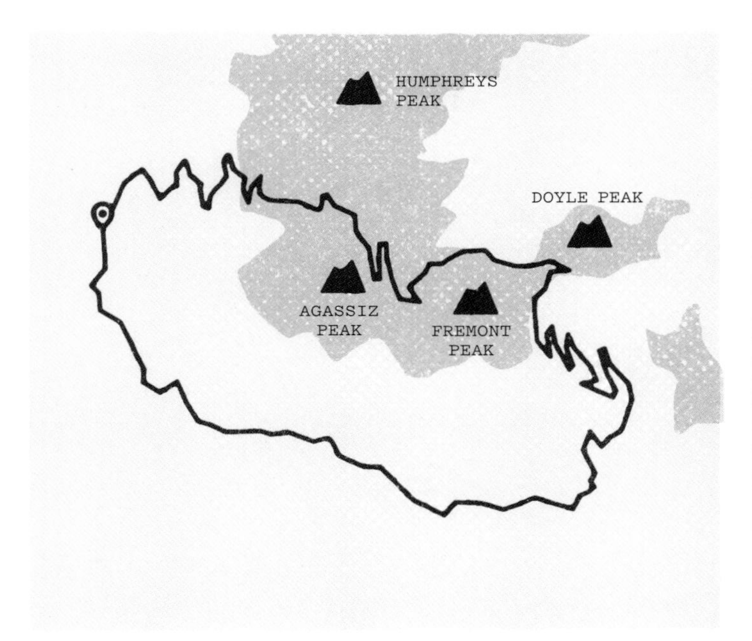

GRAND CANYON

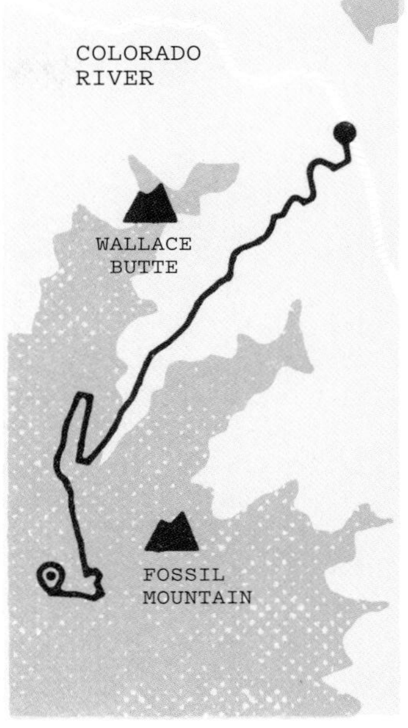

HANGOVER LOOP

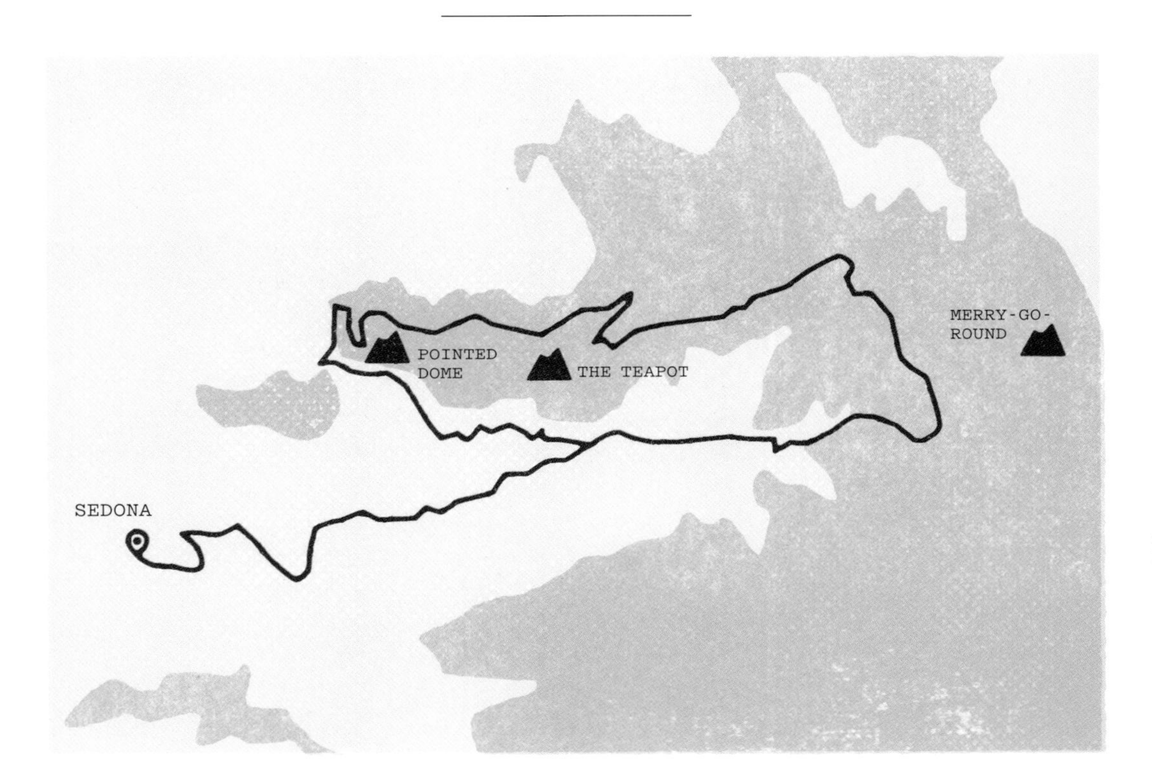

SIERRA NORTE DE OAXACA

13 | MEXICO: NORTH AMERICA

SIERRA NORTE DE OAXACA — MEXICO

Sierra Norte De Oaxaca — Mexico

THE VALLEY OF THE GHOSTS

EMMA LATHAM PHILLIPS

Featuring around 2,000 species of plant, the hauntingly beautiful landscape in the Sierra Norte is ever-changing and constantly surprising

In the Valley of the Ghosts, history is never far from view. Pine needles carpet the trail, flanked on the left by a snaking river, rushing over boulders. To the right is a tree-spangled mountain slope. Running past the rocks, tangled up in vines, you'd be forgiven for thinking you were alone – but the essence of the past is all around you.

The age of the Camino Real trail is immediately apparent, and remnants of its history trace the path through the trees. A stone bridge, out of place and centuries-old, gently crumbles into the river. Entering the Valley of the Ghosts, the trail narrows and becomes rockier. Ancient oak trees drip garlands of Spanish moss, hanging almost to the ground, silver-hued and fragile, like a wizard's beard. The landscape in the Sierra Norte is ever-changing and constantly surprising; epiphytic plants, such as tillandsias, cacti and orchids, cling to the bark of wizened trees.

In pre-Hispanic times, Mesoamerica was criss-crossed by a web of commerce routes. The Camino Real is a mountainous part of one such ancient path that connected the Gulf of Mexico to the Pacific via Oaxaca. It was used by the Zapotec communities, then the Spaniards, until, finally, it found itself a battleground during the Mexican Revolution. Today, the path is used by packhorses, ferrying people and goods between the towns of the area.

The Camino Real is one of 100km (62mi) of trails designed to connect the Pueblos Mancomunados – eight small communities in the Sierra Norte, a little-known and underappreciated mountain range in Oaxaca state. The term 'Pueblos Mancomunados' roughly translates to 'commonwealth' or 'united towns', and this region operates independently from the Mexican government.

← A group of runners tackling the trails that connect the eight Pueblos Mancomunados.

The Pueblos Mancomunados use ecotourism to share their culture with visitors while protecting their unique and hauntingly beautiful environment.

The indigenous communities control the 400,000 hectares (990,000 acres) of this mountain range. The story goes that ten Zapotec families first arrived here in search of fertile land. They never left. Now the locals are referred to as the 'People in the Clouds', owing to the winds that drag in a blanket of fog from the Gulf of Mexico. The villages are often shrouded in mist – perhaps not what you'd expect in Mexico, a country famed for sun and tequila.

Running in the Sierra Norte means negotiating a variety of microclimates, as the altitude ranges from 90m to 3,000m (300ft to 9,850ft). You'll move across subalpine grasslands, towering walls of pine and lush green deciduous forests in just one trail. The cooler temperatures and occasional veil of mist might feel more northern than southern hemisphere – until you notice the cacti and tooth-sharp agave.

It's estimated that this region is home to a whopping 2,000 plant species, and this abundance of leaf and green is never far from the trail. However, it's the so-called 'cloud forests' that are the most ethereal, where vines and ferns grow atop trees. Running through them, the rich, damp smell of moss rises from the ground and mist wets the cheek.

Benito Juárez is located just an hour and a half away from Oaxaca City. At 2,750m (9,000ft), the town is high and close to the clouds; it marks the first of the eight communities. Use the famous 150m (490ft)-long hanging bridge as a gateway to the mountains and the start of a multi-day trip between four Pueblos Mancomunados.

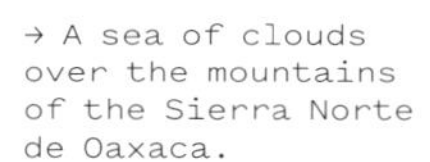

→ A sea of clouds over the mountains of the Sierra Norte de Oaxaca.

↓ Runners approaching the town of Lachatao.

On a sunny day, the hanging bridge overlooks rolling mountains; but in the mist, you feel magically suspended, wobbling over a shadowed canyon. From here, follow the dirt track down the mountain's crest. Towering above, like watchmen, are large oyamel firs and pinabete pines. Coming to a small farmhouse, a narrow and rocky footpath veers off to the left; follow it down an agave alley and pass through alpine meadows and forest. This short 8km (5mi) run features a joyful descent of about 600m (1,970ft). The last leg brings you back up to 3,050m (10,000ft) and the largest of the Pueblos Mancomunados, Cuajimoloyas.

The age of the Camino Real trail is immediately apparent, and remnants of its history trace the path through the trees. A stone bridge, out of place and centuries-old, gently crumbles into the river

It rains a lot here; the forest on the windward side receives 700–2,000mm (27–80in) of rainfall annually. But the mud and water create a playground in which runners can let loose. The route from Cuajimoloyas to Latuvi is all about fun. The drop begins gradually at first, but at about the 6km (3¾mi) mark, it becomes steep. Aim to move your feet as nimbly as possible as you scamper down the mountainside, ankles caked with mud and rocks rolling at your side. Any jackets or extra layers put on at the start of the trail will soon be whipped off.

The trail moves through a collision course of different ecosystems, which runners will speed through headlong. At 3,050m (10,000ft), the route begins in pine country, where the vibrant greens of the undergrowth and rust-red soil contrast with the deep-brown, lichen-spattered tree trunks. Look out for the

↑ A runner crosses a bridge in Benito Juárez.

→ A dirt road in the community of San Miguel Amátian.

→ Visitors can eat in the communal dining rooms (*comedor*) scattered all around the Sierra de Oaxaca, sampling fresh trout and other local, seasonal dishes.

porcupine-like cucharilla and bromeliads, with their vibrant flowers. At around 2,100m (7,000ft), the lowest point of the run, there's a noticeable change in the weather. The clouds part and the sun radiates through; it's warmer and drier. A trout farm in the river valley, Cara de León, offers freshly cooked fish, to be eaten with your fingers.

At 2,400m (8,000ft), the small town of Latuvi balances precariously across a ridge, with panoramic views at every angle. Beyond the fields of yellow maize lie endless blue peaks. At one end of the town, you'll find the picturesque Santa Martha church; this sits proudly atop the mountain, like an eagle on its nest. This pretty church is a taster of the spiritual finale to come at the end of your third and final run.

The Camino Real trail from Latuvi to Lachatao is considered by many to be the most beautiful in Oaxaca. It's 15km (9mi) long and gently rises through the mish-mash of microclimates that make the Sierra Norte unique. The path descends into an ancient tree-covered valley, meanders narrowly alongside a boulder-strewn river and passes the occasional packhorse, only to re-emerge once again on a more established road.

For those wishing to mark the end of their running journey with a bang, a temazcal can be organized in Lachatao before the return to Oaxaca City. A temazcal is a traditional Zapotec ceremony – essentially it's a steam bath in a tiny, dark adobe room, which symbolizes rebirth, healing and a return to the mother's womb. After three days spent on the track, this is a deeply cleansing experience and an opportunity to relax any aching muscles.

As I left the Valley of the Ghosts, I realized I was the last one in the group. But this didn't matter; running is not about winning, it's about everyone making it across the finish line, walking or crawling. I compelled my feet to move one in front of the other as I entered the final stretch – a cloud of dust billowed behind me on the track up to Lachatao. I gasped as I rounded the corner; there was an ornate church perched high above me, marking the end of my journey. The Santa Catarina church was built around the late sixteenth century and is regal in its design. Children played basketball in its courtyard, and I cracked open a cold beer and listened to their chatter, the condensation cooling my sweating skin.

In the deep blackness of the temazcal, I could just about make out the shapes of my fellow runners. After three days on the trails, everyone was exhausted; running pushes you to your limits and tests your strength of will. With my sight taken away, I could truly feel the weight of my body. If you're lucky enough to experience another culture, you don't often get this opportunity to look back on your trip in this way. The openness of a temazcal mirrors the ethos of the people who live in Oaxaca: considered and reflective, welcoming you with an embrace as wide and warm as this gentle blanket of steam.

→ (Opposite above): Runners feel magically suspended on the striking suspension bridge, as seen from Benito Juárez.

↓ Running in the Sierra Norte means negotiating a variety of microclimates.

↑ Shelling corn; an avocado seller at the market in Tlacolula de Matamoros; Leonor Bautista from Teotitlán del Valle, grinding grana cochinilla.

EMMA LATHAM PHILLIPS

Emma Latham Phillips is a travel and environment journalist who was first introduced to trail running through trail-running specialist travel firm Aire Libre. Typically, her days are spent writing or on the farm rather than on the track. For her, running acts as a portal to other cultures and a chance to journey through beautiful scenery. Living in Brighton means that her morning jogs are often on concrete, so she was grateful to travel to Mexico and rediscover the beauty of running in the wild. In its essence, this type of movement is deeply meditative and enables you to reconnect with your body. Her first experience of the sport was in these mountains in Oaxaca, where she combined jogging with a brisk walk. The trails described above are accessible to anyone and will forever hold a fond space in her heart.

PRACTICAL INFORMATION

Running at 3,050m (10,000ft) does have its challenges, and you may struggle with the altitude if you're not acclimatized to higher ground. Shortness of breath is a common symptom, so don't push for your personal best and slow down whenever necessary.

With the altitude comes temperature change. The higher you go, the colder it gets, and while a T-shirt might do for the lowlands, bring a coat for the peaks. Many visitors assume that Mexico is always hot, but it can reach below 10°C (50°F) here, with frequent frosts in the high mountains: remember to pack accordingly.

The rainy season is from mid-May to December, with the heaviest rains occurring between July and September. From December to May, it's drier, colder and more humid.

The accommodation in the Pueblos Mancomunados is delightful in its simplicity. The cabins are made from either brick or wood, built using local natural resources. Inside, you'll find bunks or double beds and a fire lit on a large stone hearth, crackling merrily and filling you and the room with a warm glow. More often than not, the patios outside the cabins offer breathtaking views of sweeping mountain vistas and a hammock from which to enjoy them.

All accommodation in the Pueblos Mancomunados must be booked using the official local ecotourism office, the Expediciones Sierra Norte organization. You can run the trails alone, but hiring guides and organizing a tour will provide a local's insight into the surrounding area. It's also possible to arrange private transport to Benito Juárez, or you can jump on the bus from Central de Abastos. Though the landscape is popular predominantly among hikers, a recent rise in visiting runners means it's easy to find guides who've developed a taste for the sport. In fact, you'll likely be chasing their heels.

APPROX. DISTANCE	50km (30mi)	MAXIMUM ALTITUDE	3,050m (10,000ft)	CLIMATE	altitude varies creating a range of microclimates	TERRAIN	dirt tracks; rocks; grasslands; forest
APPROX. ELEVATION	2,000m (6,560ft)	SEASON TO RUN	rainy season runs July-Sept, otherwise humid and dry	CHALLENGE LEVEL	advanced	WATCH OUT FOR	sharp changes in weather

SIERRE NORTE DE OAXACA

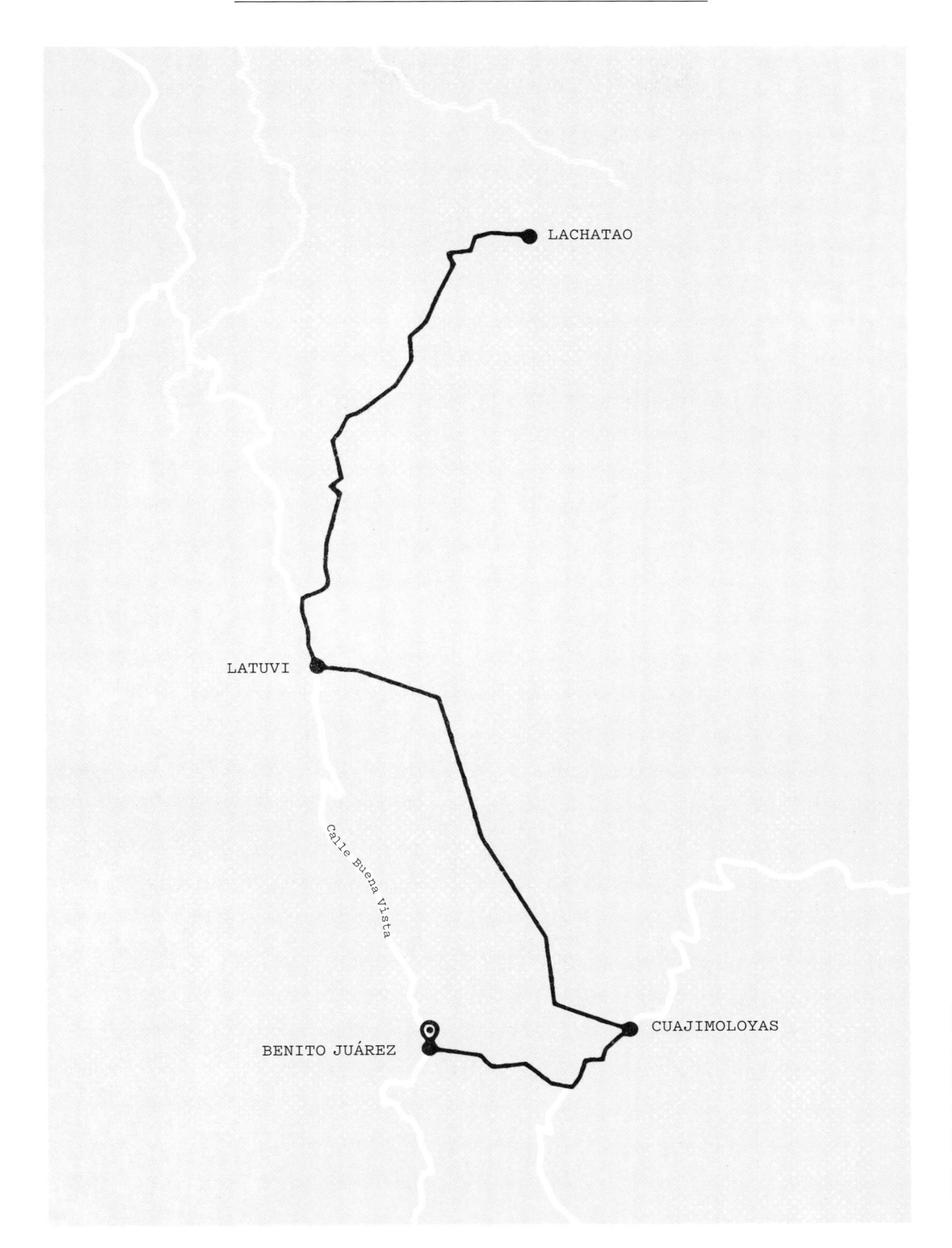

PATAGONIA

14 | CHILE: SOUTH AMERICA

PATAGONIA — CHILE

Patagonia — Chile

COMPLETE IMMERSION IN NATURE

JENNA CRAWFORD

Pumalín Park showcases the diversity of the Patagonian landscape: soft trails, dense forest, glacial rocks and breathtaking waterfalls

Gliding above the water on an old cargo ferry as it approaches Chaitén, it's easy to lose track of time as your senses become fully engaged with the beauty and expansiveness of the coastline of Patagonia. In every direction, green mountains rise out of the blue waters. The deep purple sunset becomes a backdrop to the ice-covered volcano towering over the southern portion of Pumalín Park.

Pumalín, in the Chilean Lake District, is part of South America's largest national park. Its 400,000 hectares (1,000,000 acres) are host to a diverse ecosystem of flora, including evergreen trees, ferns and thousands of other plant species, as well as to an extensive infrastructure of trails and campgrounds for public access. The park protects some of the last remaining alerce trees, also known as the Patagonian cypress, and is the home of what many people consider to be Patagonia's best trails. Travellers and hikers are drawn from all over the world to experience the magic of this remote location.

Starting 14km (8½mi) south of the town of Caleta Gonzalo, the 4km (2½mi) trail to Cascadas Escondidas (Hidden Waterfalls) begins with a steady climb through a forest of alerce trees, crossing over wooden bridges, surrounded by ferns and other vegetation, before arriving at a picturesque waterfall. The trail isn't challenging, but do stop and look around: marvel at the thick forests and listen to the sounds of rushing water as you get closer and closer to the falls.

Further along the trail, you'll notice how beautifully the sunlight filters through the thick forest and on to the ground underneath your feet. However, stay focused when navigating bridge crossings, which bounce and sway with each step. Nearer the waterfalls, watch out for slick rock. You will be able to hear the sound of the waterfall before you see it; ladder-like steps with wooden

← The enormity of sand and stone will make runners feel tiny.

handrails guide runners down into a deep, bowl-like area. The water cascades down from above, collecting in a large pool. It's an amazing spot to sit, observe and listen to the sounds of nature.

Another day-long trail showcases the diversity of the Patagonian landscape. The trailhead for the glacier-covered Michinmahuida volcano is located right off the famous Carretera Austral road, around 28km (17mi) south of Caleta Gonzalo. The terrain at the beginning of the trail is soft dirt, the 2 per cent gradient feels comfortable, and the trees and ferns build a thick canopy as you steadily ascend. The forest is so dense that it's easy to miss the volcano completely until you are much further along. The trail narrows as it penetrates deeper into the forest. Negotiating the single track can feel more like running on a tightrope – one foot in front of the other. The path becomes more technical, with large rocks, stumps and pools of water that form the glacial runoff.

The fumes of gas escaping near the summit are a reminder of the fragile balance between nature and human settlements

After 10km (6mi), the path emerges from the forest. The peak of Michinmahuida appears, although it still feels far away. The clearly defined trail disappears; runners have to navigate their own path towards the volcano, manoeuvring across the rocky ridges and loose volcanic rocks. The cool air and extraordinary views bring about a real sense of alertness and energy. Every cautious step seems to be accompanied by the sound of rock falling into the crevasse below. When you reach the base of the glacier, there's something supremely special about being able to reach forward and tentatively touch the ice.

← Runners and hikers come from all over the world to experience the magic of Patagonia.

↓ Looking out from the ferry at Corcovado volcano.

The descent follows the same path; giant nalca, also known as Chilean rhubarb, an unusual-looking plant native to southern Chile, lines the trail. It has long prickly stems and large green leaves, which can grow to 2m (6½ft) in size. It's natural to brush up against the plants during the run, but once sweat gets into those small scratches, it will sting. A dip in the river at the trailhead is the perfect end to the adventure.

Several other day hiking trails of varying lengths and difficulties start from trailheads that are easily accessible from the Caleta Gonzalo campsites.

The 10km (6mi) run to Chaitén volcano offers spectacular views of Chiloé Island on a clear and sunny day, and areas of bare trees remain as evidence of its last major eruption in 2008. Following the blast, much of the town of Chaitén was destroyed by a violent lava- and mud-flow and the river's subsequent flooding. Pumalín Park stayed closed for two years. Now, the remains of the aftermath create a fascinating contrast with all the new life that results from nature's constant revitalization. The start of the trail, Los Gigios bridge on the Southern Highway, 32.5km (20mi) south of Caleta Gonzalo, is marked with a sign that gives travellers a quick explanation of the story behind the natural disaster.

The path, mostly used for hiking, is a steep climb: more than 600m (1,970ft) of elevation gain on the way to the top of the volcano. It's a stunning 4.4km (2¾mi) round trip; basically a straight climb up on 'stairs' surrounded by lush

↑ The Sendero Paso Desolación
(Desolation Trail) takes
in the surroundings of the
imposing Osorno volcano.

↓ The region hosts a
diverse ecosystem.

vegetation and obsidian stones, finishing with 500m (1,640ft) of rock until you arrive at the rim of the crater. The fumes of gas escaping near the summit are a reminder of the fragile balance between nature and human settlements.

Even though the way to the top is hard, it is really considered 'medium difficulty' because it can be hiked using poles. It is definitely a great workout, but it's also a beautiful journey, offering an impressive panorama from the top.

Most travellers leaving Chilean Patagonia will leave Caleta Gonzalo on the ferry, and continue north by car along the Carretera Austral, towards Puerto Varas. This presents a perfect opportunity to run the Sendero Paso Desolación (Desolation Trail) in the Vicente Pérez Rosales National Park.

When you reach the base of the glacier, there's something supremely special about being able to reach forward and tentatively touch the ice

From Puerto Varas, the journey to the trailhead in Petrohué is 60km (37mi), but the coastal views, lush greenery and flowing rivers are remarkable. The trail is 12km (7½mi) one way, although this can be shortened to create an out-and-back run to the Mirador La Picada viewpoint. There is parking at the base of the trailhead, only a short walk from the shoreline of the green-blue waters of the Todos los Santos lake. The wide trail (designated 'hard' on the official map) begins with a mix of soft, deep sand and dry volcanic ash, making even the flat run feel challenging. The route begins a slow climb before a steeper, longer ascent at around 4km (2½mi). The trail crosses over multiple volcanic channels, bringing to life the notable history of Osorno volcano, which is known for its iconic cone shape and historic eruptions and lava flow. As the gradient of the trail becomes steeper, the sun-drenched route will both challenge and elate you, especially towards the viewpoint at Mirador La Picada, with its panoramic views of Todos los Santos lake and Osorno volcano, as well as several mountains further in the distance.

↑ (Above left): Dusk falling in the Cucao sector of Chiloé Island.

↑ (Above right): En route to the Michinmahuida Glacier, a place of indescribable beauty.

↑ Crossing the pampas, wetlands
and beaches in Ahuenco Park on
Chiloé Island.

During the course of my stay in Patagonia, I felt immensely grateful that my love of trail running and travel had given me the opportunity to experience the diversity of scenery and the beauty of Patagonia's forests on foot. I thought about others with whom I wished I could have shared the experience. What I came to realize was that the more I connected to myself through nature, the more I wanted to find a way for other people to do the same. At night, the blanket of stars stretched to infinity, uninterrupted by any other light. I was struck by the peacefulness – I could blame that on living in Los Angeles, a city where both the environment and the fast pace of life often leave you out of touch with nature and your own physical experience, but I couldn't think where else you would find this sort of purity in the night sky.

The trails of Patagonia brought me all the things I love about running: freedom, strength and the beautiful feeling of depletion. I developed an appreciation for being present in the moment and turning off my busy mind. Today, back in Los Angeles, I continue to nurture my passion for trail running and freedom from technology and pace statistics through mindfulness. There is tranquillity here too; I just needed to know where to look for it.

↓ (Below left): Wooden bridges are a feature of many of the area's trails.

↓ (Below right): The beautiful Chepu River at dawn.

↑ Part of the Michinmahuida Glacier.

↓ Ice from the west base of the Michinmahuida volcano, Pumalín Park.

JENNA CRAWFORD

Jenna Crawford grew up in Portland, Oregon, which is known for its long rainy season, green forests and proximity to both mountains and the coast. She picked up running later in life, after relocating to Los Angeles in 2014. Once in LA, she found herself fully immersed in road racing and quickly became part of the local running scene. Jenna is known to have a full training calendar, which favours marathon and ultra-marathon distances. However, it is the physical nature of simply running, connecting with people and travelling to new parts of the world, such as the Lake District of Patagonia, that has cemented this love of trail running. Jenna has developed her professional career in marketing in the running industry, where she helps inspire others to be active and overcome their own personal barriers through running and racing. In her free time, she enjoys writing and reading, and is a youth mentor.

PRACTICAL INFORMATION

Caleta Gonzalo is a small town on the edge of Pumalín Park, set up to host tourists and travellers, providing accommodation including a cafeteria, restaurant and campsites, and a row of quaint wooden cabins with views of the Reñihué Fjord. Near the cabins, the Caleta Gonzalo Café offers delicious homemade meals, freshly baked bread, and a small visitor centre and gift shop that stocks a selection of books, guides and maps, as well as organic honey and jams. After a day on the trails, the café offers a cosy retreat with a welcoming warm fireplace. It's the perfect place to unwind over a home-cooked dinner and a bottle of Chilean wine.

In northern Patagonia during the summer, the weather is comfortable: it is not too hot during the day, which is perfect for running, yet cool at night.

The sign for the trail to Michinmahuida volcano can easily be missed. The trail begins at Carol Urzua bridge near the base of a rainforest, next to the Río Blanco's rocky bank. The route is a 24km (15mi) round trip, but don't underestimate how long the run will take, and how hard it might prove: for hikers, this can be an eight-to-ten-hour trek. Come prepared with enough water and snacks for longer than you expect, though it's safe to drink from the perfectly clear stream you cross with around 5km (3mi) to go.

APPROX. DISTANCE	38km (24mi)	MAXIMUM ALTITUDE	2,450m (8,040ft)	CLIMATE	semi arid	TERRAIN	forest; rocks; roots
APPROX. ELEVATION	2,500m (8,200ft)	SEASON TO RUN	Nov-Feb	CHALLENGE LEVEL	mixed	WATCH OUT FOR	glacial runoff water

PUMALÍN PARK

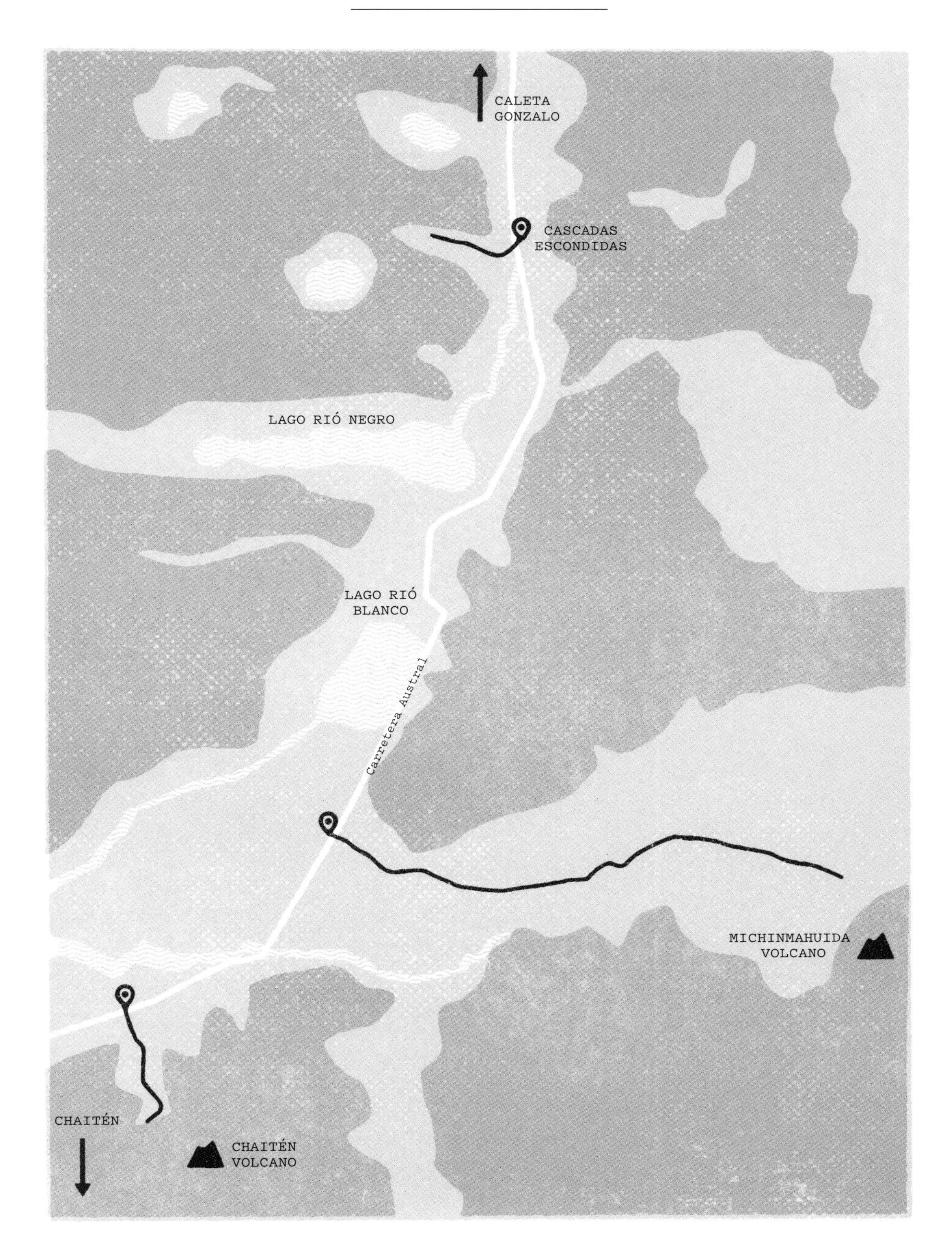

GREAT HIMALAYA TRAIL

15 | NEPAL: ASIA

Great Himalaya Trail — Nepal

THE HIGHS OF THE HIMALAYAS

LIZZY HAWKER

The many variants of this informal route link the remote and rugged districts of the highest mountain range in the world

Beautiful, rough, hard and unforgettable. On a mountain pass 5,500m (18,000ft) above sea level – a pass that in reality feels more like a summit – this is the spine of the Himalayas. This mountain range stretches for more than 2,400km (1,500mi), separating the plains of India from the Tibetan Plateau. When you stand right at the heart of it, it feels as though the world is at your feet. The wind is persistent and the atmosphere is icy cold. After this wild and isolated stretch of the Great Himalaya Trail journey, the way will finally become easier again, but in the stillness at 5,500m (18,000ft), cold, buffeted by wind, with days still ahead of you, it's tempting to think about what lies at the end of the adventure – warm food, shelter, people to talk to. The beauty and intensity of the Himalayan experience go hand in hand with its roughness and difficulty.

There *is* a line on a map. But the Great Himalaya Trail itself is, at best, a vague concept to piece together a route linking the remote and rugged mountain districts along the highest part of the Himalayan range. It's not a waymarked, defined recreational trail, such as those well-known exponents of the tag 'long-distance hiking trail' including the Appalachian Trail or the Pacific Crest Trail in the USA. Rather, the Great Himalaya Trail is an ideal, a paradigm if you will. With any number of possible variations, you choose your route to fit your purpose and intention. In reality, of course, when you are there on the ground it is anything but vague – it is tough, it is wild, it is enormous and it is humbling.

← The spectacular north face of Ama Dablam fills the sky.

The Himalayas – from the Sanskrit *hima* (snow) and *alaya* (abode) – form the highest mountain range in the world, a 2,400km (1,500mi) arc from Nanga

Parbat in the west to Namcha Barwa in the east, a physical and climatic barrier separating the monsoonal plains of the Indian subcontinent from the desert of the high Tibetan Plateau. Still growing, as the Indian tectonic plate subducts under the Eurasian plate, it is a constantly changing landscape and environment; a very real and physical reminder of the Buddhist concept of impermanence.

People have been living in these mountains for thousands of years. Trade and migration have led to an intricate network of routes and trails. And these trails were the only means of communication for a long time. Traditionally the Himalayas were traversed north to south across the main ranges by traders, shepherds and pilgrims. Crossing 5,000m (16,400ft) passes was always formidable, but it was a way of life. But these mountains and their communities were isolated from the rest of the world for years while Ladakh, Nepal, Sikkim, Bhutan and Tibet kept their borders shut to foreigners.

The beauty and intensity of the Himalayan experience go hand in hand with its roughness and difficulty

Until relatively recently, the Nepal–Tibet border regions were still restricted, so to cross Nepal required frequent detours away from the *himals* (the mountain ranges) and into the *pahirs* (mid-hills) that lie to the south of the Great Himalaya Range itself. In 2002 Nepal's *himal* regions were finally opened to permit-based trekking. The concept of a route linking the remote mountain regions of Nepal could finally be realized, and from this came the development of the Great Himalaya Trail.

↑ Numerous stone chortens above Dughla are dedicated to mountaineers.

← At 5,420m (17,780ft), the Cho La is a high pass in the Everest region connecting the Khumbu and Gokyo valleys - one of the most spectacular viewpoints in the Everest region.

Whatever route or style you choose, whether fast and in one attempt or in sections over several years, crossing the Nepal Himalayas is an incredible experience and adventure. Those making this journey through the highest mountains of the world, however they make it, learn that it is as much about the people and their mountains as it is about their own personal challenge.

Of course, there is an important caveat to our modern journeying: there is no recreational, waymarked route across the Himalayas. Instead we piece together a network of ancient local trails to suit our own goal or dream. We are there because we want to be; the local people are on the trails because they need to use them. Think about it like that and it is totally humbling.

Reaching any part of the Great Himalaya Trail takes time; given that most of the passes are higher than 5,000m (16,400ft), acclimatization needs to be factored into any trip. Unless you enter Nepal via land (from India or Tibet), then the only gateway for visitors is via the international airport in Kathmandu. It is a vast and chaotic developing city, but if you look beyond that the landscape reveals that it is also a city surrounded by a ring of hills punctuated by the four prominent summits of Shivapuri (2,731m/8,960ft) to the north, Jamacho (2,095m/6,873ft) to the north-west, Chandragiri (2,551m/8,369ft) to the south-west, and Phulchowki (2,782m/9,127ft) to the south.

For the runner, with a little effort, these hills around the Kathmandu Valley Rim offer a plethora of opportunities for all abilities. The possibilities are endless, ranging from easy day tours to multi-day challenges.

Start with a classic: a run up Shivapuri, north of the city. It's easy to reach by public transport, or by Tootle (Nepal's equivalent of Uber on motorbike). There

↑ Passing the Everest Memorial chortens during a sleepless three-day, 319km (198mi) journey with more than 10,000m (32,800ft) of ascent and descent.

are several routes to choose from and it's easy to find your way; better still, hire a Nepali runner as a guide for the day and they'll show you their favourites, as well as take you to the best place for *chiya*, *chana* and *alu* (tea, chickpeas and potato) – the perfect post-run snack.

The country is full of trails. Wherever you can walk, you can also run, and so Nepal is a true paradise for mountain and trail runners

For something longer, follow the 54km (33½mi) route of the Stupa to Stupa race, which links two of the most important Buddhist stupas in Kathmandu – from Swayambhu (nicknamed the Monkey Temple, with good reason) to Boudhanath, but taking the longer, greener way. With one big ascent at the beginning to Jamacho Gumba, the rest of the route is on beautiful, mostly runnable trails through pine forests skirting the edge of the valley rim. How better to get to know Kathmandu than looking upon it from above via five monasteries and one hermit's cave?

Then, of course, there is the ultimate, near-160km (100mi) circumnavigation of the entire valley rim (also increasingly attempted as an individual challenge 'round' in the style of the Bob Graham Round in the English Lake District). The trails offer a wonderfully varied landscape, from jungle forest

to ridge trails to paddy fields. On a clear day it's even possible to see the 'big' mountains, from Manaslu and Annapurna to Ganesh Himal, Jugal Himal and Langtang Himal. Take your time and do it over four days, or challenge yourself to complete it in one.

The trail-running culture has grown dramatically in Nepal during the past decade or two, as it has worldwide. But Nepal is special: as a developing nation, its road network has only recently extended into the hill and mountain regions. For the most part, to reach anywhere you had to walk – hence the country is full of trails. Wherever you can walk, you can also run, and so Nepal is a true paradise for mountain and trail runners.

← A clear evening sky above Kathmandu reveals the majestic Ganesh Himal range.

↓ Trail runner Lizzy Hawker has completed the Great Himalaya Trail solo twice.

We all have one. It is *that* run. It is where we go in the cool of the early morning, in the heat of the day, in the fading light of a setting sun. It is a place we go to in all seasons, observing and feeling the changes, until the rhythm of the earth becomes our own, a comforting reminder of the impermanence of all things.

My bicycle is the conduit that channels me between the chaotic streets of Kathmandu and freedom. The cycle jolts me out of morning inertia and the tide of life sweeps me along with it until the city has dwindled into the paddy fields at the foot of the Shivapuri hills.

Even with the first step I'm shaken into a stillness. The turmoil of emotion that permeates my every day is held in suspension. There is a quiet within my movement. I think. But my thoughts are not my master. For the moment I am simply running. Identity and purpose are irrelevant. To be running is enough. Because if I am running then I am alive. And to be alive is everything.

I know how it will feel beneath my feet, I know where there will be mud even on the hottest day, I know which rocks I will slip on and which not, I know which branch to grab to break a descent or ease a step up. I know it green and lush in the post-monsoon fecundity, I know it in the winter, sparse and dry.

It is *that* run. It is the run that both sets me free and brings me back home.

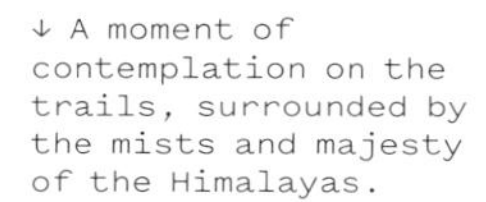

↓ A moment of contemplation on the trails, surrounded by the mists and majesty of the Himalayas.

↑ Welcoming tea houses at Kyanjin Gompa glow under a night sky along the Great Himalaya Trail.

↓ Nepal is a true paradise for mountain and trail runners.

LIZZY HAWKER

On foot whenever possible, as an elite British athlete Lizzy Hawker held the world record for twenty-four hours on the road and won the Ultra-Trail du Mont-Blanc an unprecedented (and unmatched) five times. She first visited Nepal in 2007 to climb Ama Dablam (6,812m/22,349ft) and to attempt to run from Everest Base Camp back to Kathmandu. She repeated this 'run' twice and still holds the record (63 hours 8 minutes). She has twice crossed the Nepal Himalayas solo along the Great Himalaya Trail and is a *National Geographic* Adventurer of the Year and now race director of the Ultra Tour Monte Rosa. Her passion for exploring is taking her far beyond competition to high, wild places - often alone, and often in Nepal. Author of *Runner* and a scientist by training, Lizzy is also part of the teaching team on the Movement, Mind and Ecology MA at Schumacher College, England.

PRACTICAL INFORMATION

According to the 'Thru hiker database' maintained by Himalayan Adventure Labs, as of spring 2020, the Nepal section had seen ninety-seven 'Full Nepal GHT' crossings and many other expeditions and notable efforts. The most popular seasons are spring (April/May) and autumn (October/November), with the summer monsoon and winter snows bringing their own challenges. Just as there is variety in route choice, so there is in style – solo trekking, guided tea house trek or camping trek. Your choice will be guided by your route, budget, time and personal preference.

Trail Running Nepal, an informal organization formed to help develop the sport in Nepal, to encourage local participation and to offer support to Nepali trail runner athletes, is a wonderful resource for advice, inspiration and a race calendar, as well as to find news about Nepali athletes. There are now many single- and multi-stage races throughout the year, and there is a growing and increasingly enthusiastic community of runners (Nepali and expat) who are eager to share their trails with visitors. Namaste!

APPROX. DISTANCE	64km (40mi)	MAXIMUM ALTITUDE	higher than 5,000m (16,400ft)	CLIMATE	warmer at the base of the mountains; snow and ice the higher you climb	TERRAIN	rocks; mud; forest; ridges; paddy fields
APPROX. ELEVATION	3,000m (9,800ft)	SEASON TO RUN	Apr-May & Oct-Nov	CHALLENGE LEVEL	expert	WATCH OUT FOR	take time to acclimatize to the altitude

SHIVAPURI PEAK

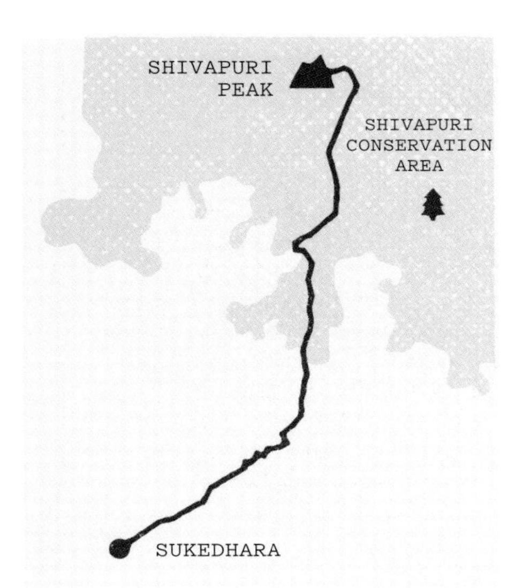

STUPA TO STUPA

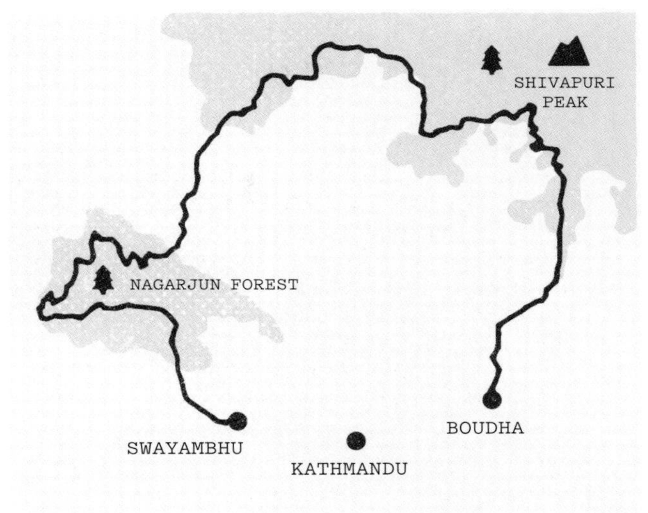

KATHMANDU VALLEY RIM

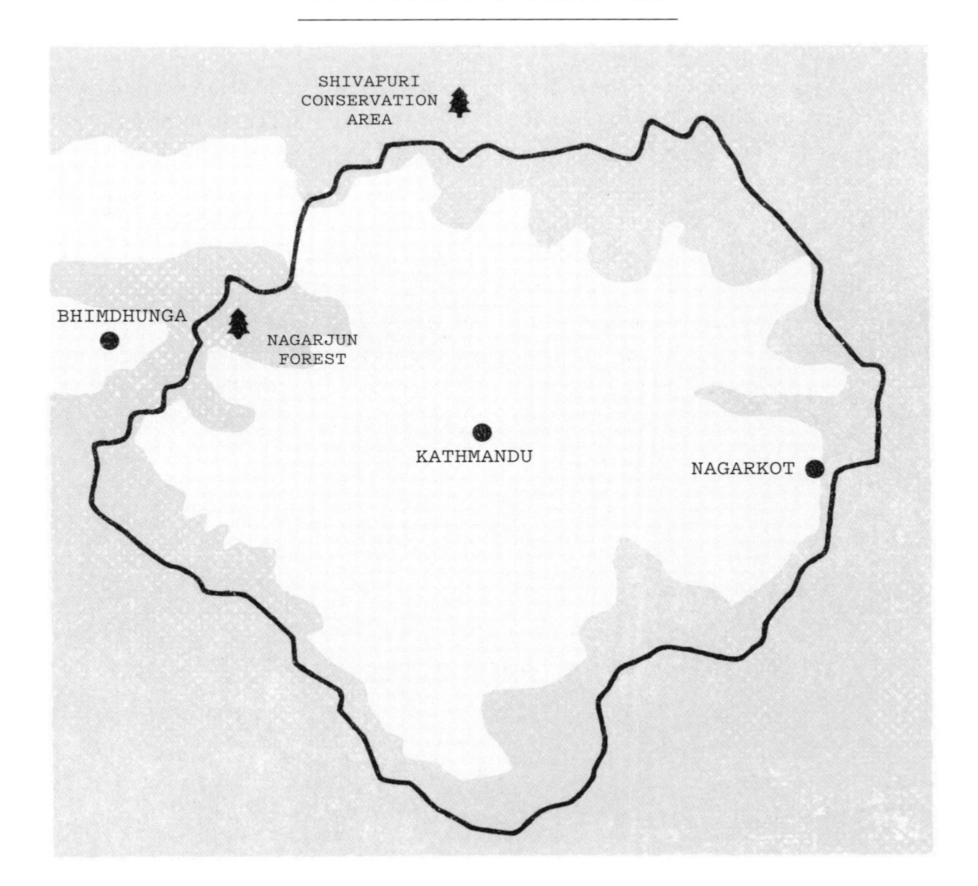

THE WEST MACDONNELL RANGES

16 | NORTHERN TERRITORY: AUSTRALIA

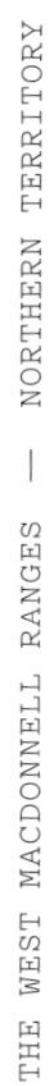

The West MacDonnell Ranges — Northern Territory

SOLITUDE IN THE OUTBACK

TOM LE LIEVRE

Among the remote gorges, sandy riverbeds and jagged ridgelines of the West MacDonnell Ranges lies the stunning Larapinta Trail

← Desert grasslands, backed by wavy ridges rolling into the distance.

Standing on top of a ridge in the West MacDonnell Ranges, what's striking is the deep sense of nothingness, stretching out for hundreds, thousands of kilometres. But also nothingness inside. Runners who make it to this part of Australia's Northern Territory leave the stress, expectations and chaos of the outside world behind. The cool breeze, the soft winter sun and the only noise to contend with being the gentle crunch of rocky trail underfoot make the Larapinta Trail a runner's delight.

The West MacDonnell National Park (known as Tjoritja to the local Aboriginal people), part of the MacDonnell Ranges, stretches out from Alice Springs, finishing some 160km (100mi) later. Made up of jagged ridgelines, deep, remote gorges and sandy riverbeds, the range houses one of Australia's premium multi-day walking trails, the Larapinta.

Snaking across the outback, the Larapinta covers an uninterrupted stretch of rocky terrain, broken up by rough gorges that house life-giving waterholes. Dry riverbeds sit dormant, waiting for the summer rains. Tall, strong eucalyptus trees cling to the edges of the empty rivers, signs that water can be found if you bury roots deep enough.

This ancient landscape has been mostly untouched for millennia. Apart from a two-lane road, some buildings here and there and the odd camel (brought over during the early 1900s before motorized transport was introduced), the signs of human interference are limited, and a true feeling of wilderness still exists.

The Larapinta presents a great opportunity for the 'rough-it' multi-day adventurers out there, for van-lifers – and also for those who would prefer a beer and soft bed after a long day's exploring. Those looking for the latter will find Glen Helen resort the ideal choice. It features a restaurant, hotel rooms, bunks and a campsite, as well as the all-important bar.

Glen Helen is called a resort, but take this with a pinch of salt. Originally a lodge that was part of a cattle ranch, Glen Helen has been transformed into a 'resort' while maintaining authentic outback charm. Don't expect five-star luxury, but do expect an unforgettable outback experience. Glen Helen backs on to the Finke River, believed to be the world's oldest riverbed.

Once on the summit, the wait for sunrise begins: the band of light builds and builds until the sun suddenly spills over the horizon

An excellent single-day run stretches 26km (16mi) and focuses on a stunning stretch of water. Dramatically cutting through the seemingly impenetrable walls of the West MacDonnell Ranges, Ormiston Gorge is one of the most beautiful gorges along the Larapinta. It's easily accessible with any vehicle, plus there's camping and even a (seasonal) kiosk to get cold drinks and snacks.

From the Ormiston Gorge car park, there's easy access to the Pound Walk, so named because it offers excellent views over the Pound, a rectangular mountain range with a flat, rocky basin. Following along the ridgeline, the route drops down into the basin before following a dusty trail to reach Ormiston Gorge, where clearly defined trails transition into a rocky riverbed, and finally into slabs that have been polished by the summer rains. There's shelter in the shade of the walls of the gorge, made up of layered sheets of rock forced on top of one another by geological movement millennia ago, almost giving the appearance of stacked-up dried slices of bread, crumbed by time.

Weary runners can wash off the sweat of the previous few hours by taking a dip in the cold water of Ormiston Gorge before heading off on the next part of the adventure.

↑ Pause, take a breath and enjoy the moment.

← (Opposite left): Crystal-clear blue skies await runners during the winter months.

← (Left): Technical sections mean runners can't drop their guard.

The trail winds out of the gorge, stopping at Hilltop lookout, which reveals the first glimpse of Mount Sonder, a solitary mountain that punctures the plane of the desert floor. From here on the trail flattens out slightly and meanders along, crossing riverbeds, ridges and the occasional cluster of eucalyptus that has found a rare patch of moisture.

Eventually the route arrives at the Finke River campsite, where there are two options: spending the night at the camp or following the access trail to Glen Helen. (This will add approximately 5km/3mi to your day's running.)

The second day's run covers the 31km (19mi) between Glen Helen and Redbank. Early risers will be rewarded with a spectacular sunrise as they head out on to section 11 of the Larapinta.

This section isn't the most strenuous, but it is beautiful. In the distance, Mount Sonder, the final objective, draws closer and closer with every step as the trail winds its way across the rocky ground.

The final day's adventure is the climb up Mount Sonder (or Rwetyepme, to give it its Aboriginal name), the Northern Territory's fourth-highest mountain. At a modest 1,380m (4,527ft), it's by no means big; however, its charm cannot be denied. Reaching up to the sky from the desert floor, it's described in Aboriginal culture as being 'a pregnant woman on her back'.

Runners embarking on this 16km (10mi) adventure will best experience Sonder by setting off a few hours before dawn, with head-torches. Starting

↑ The West MacDonnells offer endless, rolling ridgelines to explore.

at Redbank Gorge in the crisp morning desert air, your head-torch restricting your view to the experience happening directly at your feet, the slow climb to the summit is tremendous. The first glimpse of light begins to reveal the arid, rocky terrain of the surrounding landscape. Once on the summit, the wait for sunrise begins: the band of light builds until the sun spills over the horizon, slowly spreading itself across the open plains and washing down the sides of ridges that run off into the distance.

Once you've sat for long enough and pondered your existence, it's time for the fun part ... a beautiful 8km (5mi) downhill. It's fast, but be careful: one false step could mean a fall on to excruciatingly hard ground.

Following the death-defying descent, there's no better antidote than sipping a cold beer and taking it all in. If you're lusting for more, it's there, in the West MacDonnells – just get out and explore.

For anyone who prefers to rough it and enjoys the discomfort of sleeping on the ground after a long day running, it's possible to link these sections together in one multi-day push. This route will reduce your overall running distance by 10km (6mi) (63km/39mi total) as there's no need for the out-and-back to Glen Helen. However, it will require a few additional considerations as you will need to be far more self-reliant. It's not for the inexperienced: this will take some planning, given the route is in the middle of nowhere. However, a day spent setting up food drops should suffice. Another option is to use a local tour company that specializes in Larapinta Trail logistics, such as Trek Support.

↑ Piercing the desert floor, Mount Sonder, the runner's final objective, reveals itself.

← Atop a ridge that resembles the crest of a wave.

→ Eucalyptus trees cling to the edges of empty rivers.

↑ Even though the Larapinta Trail is well established, a true feeling of wilderness still exists.

→ A natural archway, creased by millennia of geological activity.

The scale of the West MacDonnell Ranges was really brought home to me while out on a day's running to Waterfall Gorge, a remote area on section 9 of the trail. After scrambling through Inarlanga Pass, a boulder-filled area scattered with cycads, I took a moment to rest in the shade, the air chilled by the rocks releasing the cool breeze they had stored from the previous night. I headed out into the next open, rocky area, towering ridgelines in the distance. The sun was high in the sky, and waves of heat blurred the horizon. From afar I noticed movement. Slowly, five hikers came into view. We stopped to talk and they explained that I was the first person they had seen in five days.

It dawned on me that this place was so remote, so untouched, that if I were simply to take a few steps off the trail, I would likely be placing my feet on ground on which no other human had stood.

The Larapinta holds a special place in my heart. Every experience I had on that trail is stored in my memory a decade later, triggered by moments I experience now. Every ridge I stand on, every crunch my foot makes on a rocky trail, every cool breeze that gently plays with my hair, every warm spring day or clear, starry sky takes me back to those formative years in my running. Reminding me about what's important and why I run.

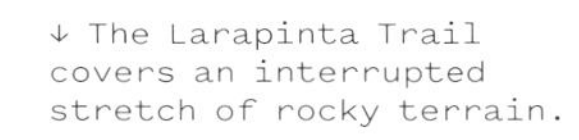

↓ The Larapinta Trail covers an interrupted stretch of rocky terrain.

MEET THE GUIDE

TOM LE LIEVRE

Born and raised in the hills of southern England, Tom Le Lievre found his passion for trail running in his twenties while backpacking around Australia. He was given the opportunity to live and work in a small resort in Central Australia that happened to back on to one of Australia's most spectacular hiking trails. On days off with nothing to do (it was 130km/81mi to the nearest town), he began to cure his boredom by exploring a section of the Larapinta, and soon fell in love with running as a way to discover new areas.

After years of running and exploring, Tom moved back to the UK. He turned his passion into a career and now works as a running coach, helping others to achieve goals and to reach their true potential.

PRACTICAL INFORMATION

These runs require some logistics: Ormiston–Glen Helen requires a drop-off at Ormiston Gorge or collection at Glen Helen. Glen Helen–Redbank Gorge requires pickup at Redbank Gorge. At the Finke River campsite there is water (in tanks) and a raised/covered sleeping area (first come, first served).

Out on the trail, water is going to be your biggest consideration. Permanent water is rare on the trail and, even then, can become stagnant over the winter months. There are water tanks at each trailhead, as well as some placed intermittently on sections of the trail. These are maintained by the park rangers and filled regularly. Note, though, that this is bore water and will have a strong mineral taste. It's advisable to treat this water. For the run described here, there are water tanks at Ormiston Gorge, Finke River, Rockbar Gap and Redbank Gorge. Even in winter, temperatures can reach 30°C+ (86°F+), so hydration remains a key consideration.

For the multi-day run, you will need to leave food caches at Finke River and Redbank in order to resupply after each day's running. These need to be dingo-proof, as canine opportunists will happily swipe supplies and leave you stranded with nothing to eat. And it's not just your edibles that need protecting: dingoes have been known to chew boots left outside tents – they really will eat anything.

Each trailhead has a designated campsite. It's not uncommon to experience sub-zero temperatures through the winter months, so make sure your sleeping gear is up to the task.

Camping/van life is also a great option. Alice Springs has rental companies that offer vans and cars; the only downside to this option is that you will have difficulty completing point-to-point sections without arranging transport to collect you or drop you off.

APPROX. DISTANCE	73km (45mi)	MAXIMUM ALTITUDE	1,380m (4,527ft)	CLIMATE	extreme differences, from monsoons to extreme heat	TERRAIN	rocky; gorges; sandy riverbeds
APPROX. ELEVATION	1,200m (3,900ft)	SEASON TO RUN	May–Aug	CHALLENGE LEVEL	expert	WATCH OUT FOR	dingoes; limited water supply

LARAPINTA TRAIL

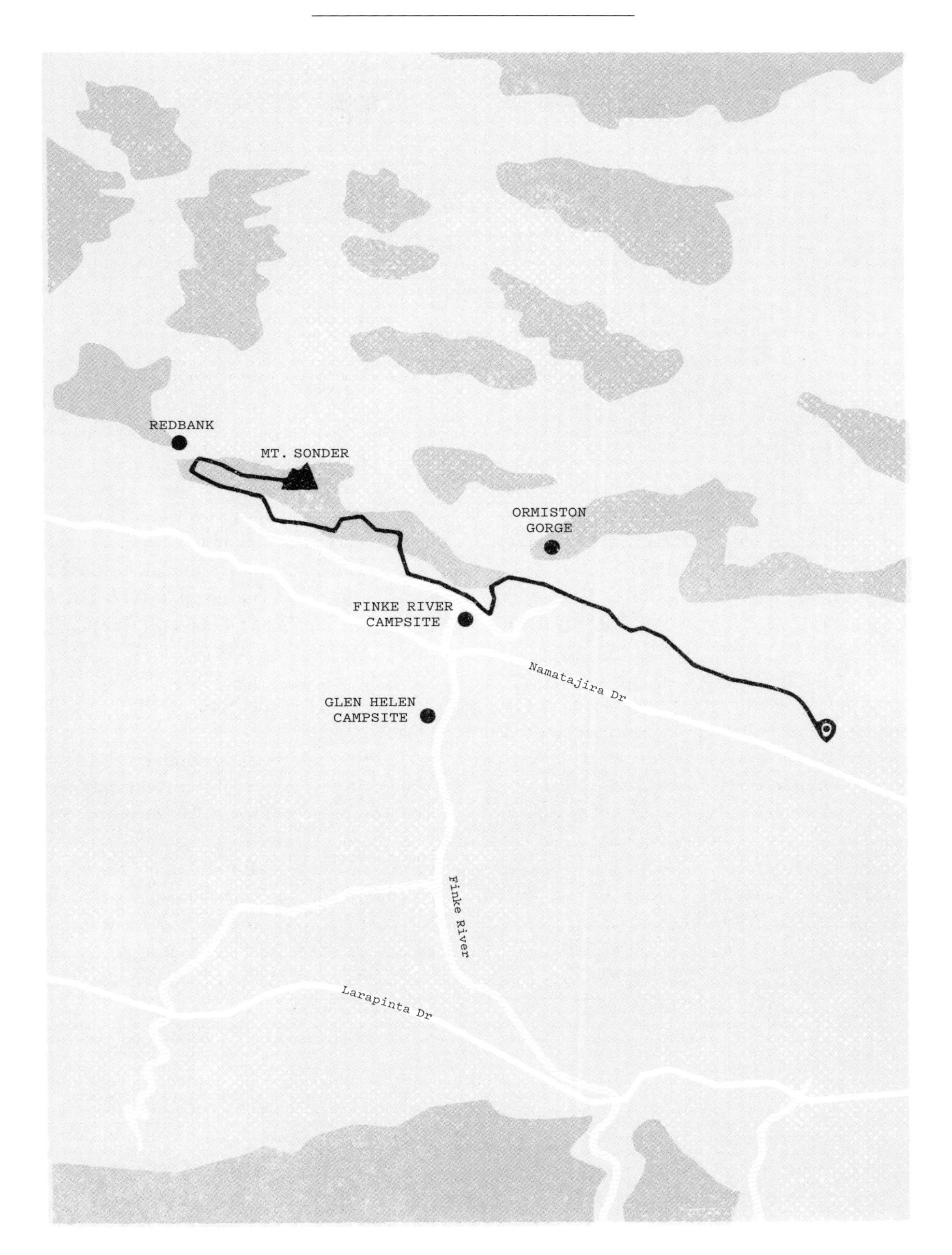

↑ (Previous pages): Prayer flags frame the view from the top of Kyanjin Ri in the Langtang Valley in the Himalayas.

← The Aiguilles de Bavella massif in Corsica.

TIPS ON THE GROUND

We hope that the amazing destinations in this book have inspired you to hit the trails. But inspiration is just part of the recipe for an incredible experience. Preparation is vital, too. So we have come up with a few notes on the practical aspects of trail running that will help to ensure that you have the best possible time.

COVERING THE GROUND:

As you will have read in many of the chapters, trails are a shared space. Others will be moving at a different pace from you. This book is all about trail running. But the reality is that trail running sits at one end of a spectrum of pedestrianism that includes hiking or backpacking at the opposite end and fastpacking somewhere in the middle. When we refer to hiking and backpacking, we're talking about setting out with the specific aim to walk from one place to another. Hikers don't worry about minimizing weight to the same degree that runners do, and will usually carry more equipment (perhaps a tent and cooking stuff, for example) and wear sturdier and more supportive footwear. Runners, on the other hand, tend to keep weight as low as possible – so that would mean trainers, not boots, and a small pack containing the bare minimum. In between those two, we have fastpackers. Fastpacking refers to the idea of moving fast in the mountains with lightweight kit and equipment, but not as stripped back as for a runner. By the way, we're not advocating that running is better than any other form of using your feet to move along the trail. And in fact, it might be that you will fastpack, hike and run at different times. The main point is to be out on the trails, making the most of nature. Just remember to set yourself up for the conditions and terrain you are going to encounter.

FITNESS PLAYS A PART:

As far as possible, we have tried to offer a range of lengths of trails and levels of difficulty in this book. However, everyone's fitness levels and experience will be unique – and you should choose your adventures accordingly. Each of the trails has been assigned a 'Challenge Level', and fits into one of four categories:

→ **Beginner:** Ideal for runners who want to test out their trail legs on moderate terrain that offers plenty of options for rest and very light levels of technicality.

→ **Advanced:** Suited to those with some previous trail running or fastpacking experience, who feel at ease in an unknown location and medium levels of technicality, but don't want to be exposed to challenging conditions.

→ **Expert:** Reserved for seasoned trail runners with previous mountain experience, who are willing to be exposed to challenging conditions and/or very technical trails.

→ **Mixed (open to anyone):** Those destinations offer a range of challenges for all abilities, from easy trails for beginners to technical terrain and mountain routes for experienced trail runners.

In places such as Chamonix (see pp.42–55) and the White Mountains (see pp.152–67) there are options for beginners and more experienced runners alike, whereas in Australia (see pp.224–37) or the Himalayas (see pp.210–23), the conditions and remoteness of the trails mean they are not ideal for first-timers. Our aim with this book is to inspire you to get out and to have a great experience moving in nature. To that end, be honest with how fit and capable you are. It is always better to start with something less challenging and work your way up rather than bite off too much in the first place and have a bad time.

PLANNING AHEAD:

Whether you are new to trail running or an old hand, having the right footwear, clothing and equipment will make all the difference to your adventure. The basics for a short outing in good conditions on non-technical trails are trail-specific running shoes (which offer good grip and some protection from stones, rocks and roots) plus comfortable running apparel. Once you go beyond that, you should consider adding to your equipment and clothing where necessary.

→ The right clothing is not only going to add to your comfort – it can make you much safer. If there is a chance that you'll find cold and wet conditions on the trails, then wear or carry waterproof and warm gear. A lightweight jacket and trousers will fit easily into a bag so, even if the conditions look great when you start, it's better to carry a little additional weight than to get caught out.

→ A pack is pretty much essential for all but the shortest trail runs. Vest-style packs are very popular. They hug your back, which means minimal bounce (much more comfortable than a traditional backpack) and come with multiple pockets to stash all the additional items you'll need.

→ In your pack it is worth carrying certain items that can make your adventure safer and more comfortable. Something to eat and drink is crucial for runs where you might be out for a few hours or more – there are energy bars to suit every diet and taste. And while a litre of water will add weight, it is a good idea to take a drink. Use a bladder that sits in your backpack or a couple of bottles to ensure the weight is evenly distributed.

→ Taking a safety blanket, a whistle, a torch and a fully charged mobile phone (all stored in something waterproof) means that if you do encounter any problems, you have the means to summon help and be protected from the elements.

We also recommend to everyone heading out on the trails that you tell someone where you are going and how long you think you are likely to be. If that is not possible, then leave a note with those details where someone looking for you can easily find it.

Whatever the weather, it is always worth planning ahead and checking the forecast. There are occasions, in the wilder parts of the planet, when reacting to a predicted change in the weather means that altering, postponing or even cancelling your plans is the right thing to do. If in doubt, talk to a local who can advise you.

As we mentioned in the introduction to this book, many of the most beautiful, life-affirming and fulfilling trails also happen to be in the most fragile and at-risk parts of the planet. It is worth reiterating that here. We want people to get out and enjoy the trails. But we also believe that those visiting the world's most stunning natural areas have a responsibility to them. At the very minimum, you must ensure that you do not leave anything behind. If you carry it on to the trails, you should carry it off them too. Litter is a blight no matter where it is found, but on the trails it is inexcusable.

We also believe that in many parts of the world, where the landscape is under threat, it is important to stick to the trails. That can mean not running even a metre to the left or right. Once soil erosion away from the established trail starts, it can cause huge damage to the delicate natural balance.

Unfortunately, no book on trail running would be complete without a mention of toilet etiquette. If you need to urinate, the advice is to make sure you are at least 70m (230ft) from any water sources. And if you need to use paper, put it in a Ziploc bag when you are done and take it with you to be disposed of when you are able to. Don't burn the paper – that is unnecessary and dangerous, especially if you are in an area prone to wildfires.

For more solid toilet requirements, this will depend on where you are. In some high-altitude, particularly sensitive areas, or those with a lot of visitors, there can be a requirement to take what you produce with you. You can buy bags specifically for this use, so check ahead to know if you'll need them. If you don't have to take your waste with you, then the best thing to do is find a spot at least 70m (230ft) from any water sources, campsites or trails. If possible, choose a sunny site with loose soil (sunlight helps to break down organic material). Dig a hole – known as a cat hole – at least 10cm (4in) deep. Do what you need to and then cover the hole with the earth you removed. Pack your used toilet paper in a Ziploc bag – which needs to be taken with you and disposed of appropriately. If you find yourself in an area where digging a hole is not possible, then lifting a rock and replacing it when you are finished is acceptable.

When it comes to cleaning your hands – which, of course, is important – use hand sanitizer and/or antibacterial wipes. And then – you guessed it! – take any wipes you use with you. Do not use soap, not even biodegradable soap, especially in rivers, where it will harm aquatic life.

ENCOUNTERS ON THE TRAIL:

There are two main encounters that can happen on the trail – wildlife and other people. In general, wildlife will know that you are coming long before you reach them. But if you do encounter any animals on the trail, remember that you are a visitor in their home. At the very least, slow to a walk – or, better still, stop and let whatever you have come across go about its business. Of course, different rules may apply if what you meet on the trails can be dangerous (see p.150 on the trails in Canada for some discussion around this). If you are going running in a place where the wildlife could be a risk, do your research before you go, learn what to do if you have an encounter on the trail and acquire anything you need before you set off.

And then, of course, there are other humans. It is good etiquette to give way to someone coming uphill if the path is too narrow for you to pass comfortably. If you are approaching someone who is going in the same direction as you, slow down – even to a walk – to pass them. No one wants to be scared out of their wits as they immerse themselves in nature. And, whichever way you are passing someone, offer a friendly wave and perhaps say hello. We also think that, as with the custom in Sweden, keeping the volume low is usually appropriate – many people hit the trails for the solitude and calmness, so respect that. Generally, we believe that you should give others on the trail the space and quiet to enjoy their adventure in peace.

Of course, it is also always the case that if you encounter someone who appears to be in difficulty or is lost, you should check whether there is anything you can do for them. Be polite and don't be offended if you are told that your assistance is not required. It is always better to check and continue on your way than to pass by someone who might need help.

The final piece of advice we would offer here is to say that wherever possible you should respect the local people you meet on the trail or in the places you pass through. An area's customs and traditions are vitally important and part of what makes each place special. So read up and do some research on where you are going before you get there. Buy from local traders and eat in local restaurants if you can. If you need a guide, try to find someone who lives in the region you are visiting. Take part in local customs, if possible and appropriate. Your experience will be all the richer as a result.

To put yourself in the best possible position to have an amazing adventure, use your common sense, do some research and take adequate precautions. We hope we'll see you on the trails soon.

RACES AND USEFUL WEBSITES

GENERAL

www.likethewindmagazine.com/runningwild

The *Running Wild* companion website, where you can access more information about this book, its destinations and up-to-date insider tips.

www.likethewindmagazine.com/ltwtv

The *Running Wild* curated film library, an ever-evolving repository of the best trail-running inspiration.

THE DOLOMITES

www.dolomiti.org/en

Official tourism website for the Dolomites, complete with all the information required to organize a trip.

www.ultratrail.it/en

The Lavaredo Ultra Trail website covers the race series, with options from 20km (12mi) to 120km (75mi).

THE LOFOTEN ISLANDS

www.lofotenislands.no

Official tourism website for the Lofoten Islands, with all the necessary information and things to do.

www.lofotenskyrace.no

A race with distances ranging from 10km (6mi) to 32km (20mi) on the main island.

www.thearctictriple.no

The Arctic Triple is a race between 12km (7.5mi) and 161km (100mi) in the midnight sun.

THE CHAMONIX VALLEY

www.autourdumontblanc.com/en

Tourism website for the Tour du Mont Blanc, with extensive practical information and bookable accommodation.

www.utmbmontblanc.com

One of the biggest and most high-profile ultra-trail races in the world.

INVERIE & THE KNOYDART PENINSULA

www.trailrunningscotland.com

Guide to trail running in Scotland, including training camps and guided runs.

www.airelibre.run

Guided trips to some of the most beautiful trails in the world, including Knoydart.

www.ultra-x.co/scotland-125

Two-day trail stage race over 125km (78mi) in the Scottish Highlands (with an option to race 50km (30mi) on the second day).

CORSICA

www.pnr-resa.corsica

The Corsica National Park website allows you to discover and book refuges for your stay in Corsica.

www.restonicatrail.fr

A race in Corsica with options from 17km (10.5mi) to 110km (68mi).

www.corsicacoastrace.com

Choose whether you want to race over three or six stages, covering between 41km (25mi) and 155km (96mi).

THE PYRENEES

www.spain.info/en/nature/ordesa-monte-perdido-national-park

Useful website packed with information about the Ordesa and Monte Perdido National Park in Spain.

www.ultrapirineu.com/en

Race in the Pyrenees with options from 20km (12mi) to 100km (62km), and a vertical kilometre for those so inclined.

www.psr.run/en

A seven-stage race taking in 240km (149mi) in the Pyrenees.

THE KUNGSLEDEN

www.visitsweden.com/where-to-go/northern-sweden/swedish-lapland/kings-trail-kungsleden

Official tourism site for The Kungsleden, packed with practical information for visitors.

www.swedishlapland.com/stories/kings-trail

A race following the exact route described in this book (see page 98).

www.emelieforsberg.com/kungsleden-completed
Ultra-trail runner Emelie Forsberg set a Fastest Known Time (FKT) for the Kungsleden in 2018. This is the story of that record-breaking run.

THE LAKE DISTRICT

www.lakedistrict.gov.uk
Official tourism website, full of tips and advice on how to make the most of a trip to the Lake District.

www.lakelandtrails.org
Races throughout the year including a 100km (62mi) ultra in the summer.

www.fellrunner.org.uk
The ultimate guide to the sport of fell running, including links to dozens of races.

JURA

www.j3l.ch/en
The official guide to the area, full of information and inspiration.

www.swisscanyontrail.com
A race in the Jura with options from 31km (19mi) to 111km (69mi).

BRITISH COLUMBIA

www.britishcolumbia.com
Official tourism guide to British Columbia, with links for things to do, accommodation and places to visit.

www.5peaks.com/britishcolumbia
Summer race series with options from 5km (3mi) to 100km (62mi).

THE WHITE MOUNTAINS

www.visitwhitemountains.com
All the information you need to plan a trip to the White Mountains.

SEDONA & FLAGSTAFF

www.natra.org
The Northern Arizona Trail Runners Association promotes trail running in northern Arizona, as well as organizing weekly trail runs.

www.aravaiparunning.com
Arizona-based trail race organizer.

SIERRE NORTE DE OAXACA

www.sierranorte.org.mx
Practical guide to the trails and visitor highlights in Oaxaca's Sierra Norte.

www.airelibre.run
Guided trips to some of the most beautiful trails in the world, including Oaxaca.

PATAGONIA

www.patagoniarun.com/en
Trail race in Patagonia with distances from 10km (6mi) to 160km (100mi).

www.airelibre.run
Guided trips to some of the most beautiful trails in the world, including Patagonia.

GREAT HIMALAYA TRAIL

www.welcomenepal.com
Official tourism website for the whole of Nepal.

www.greathimalayatrail.com
Guide to the Great Himalaya Trail, with all the necessary practical information and helpful cultural considerations.

https://trailrunningnepal.org
Website set up to promote trail running in Nepal and support Nepali athletes, with links to dozens of races.

www.manaslutrailrace.org
A seven-day stage race that covers 130km (81mi), including a pass 5,000m (16,400ft) above sea level.

THE WEST MACDONNELL RANGES

www.larapintatrail.com.au
The official tourism guide to the Larapinta Trail, with all the information needed to organize a trip.

https://runlarapinta.rapidascent.com.au
Details for a four-day, four-stage trail race on the Larapinta Trail.

BIBLIOGRAPHY

OUT AND BACK: A RUNNER'S STORY OF SURVIVAL AGAINST ALL ODDS

HILLARY ALLEN

In 2017, professional ultra-runner Hillary Allen fell 45m (150ft) from a mountain ridge, suffering multiple broken bones, including a fractured back. This book reveals her fight to heal, rebuild and return to running.

BEYOND IMPOSSIBLE: FROM RELUCTANT RUNNER TO GUINNESS WORLD RECORD BREAKER

MIMI ANDERSON

When stay-at-home mother-of-three Mimi Anderson took up running in her thirties, she had little idea she would claim multiple Guinness World Records.

FEET IN THE CLOUDS: THE CLASSIC TALE OF FELL-RUNNING AND OBSESSION

RICHARD ASKWITH

Richard Askwith spent an entire season running as many of the major fell races as possible, culminating in the Bob Graham Round: a non-stop circuit of forty-two of the Lake District's highest peaks to be completed within twenty-four hours. This is his story.

GRAND TRAIL: A MAGNIFICENT JOURNEY TO THE HEART OF ULTRARUNNING AND RACING

FREDERIC BERG AND ALEXIS BERG

In *Grand Trail*, brothers and long-time *Like the Wind* magazine friends Frederic and Alexis Berg (who also photographed the Dolomites, Lofoten and Flagstaff in *Running Wild*), follow the greats of the ultra-running world, with intimate interviews and breathtaking photography.

GET TO THE SUNSHINE: LIFE LESSONS THAT BROUGHT ME TO THE WESTERN STATES FINISH LINE

LAURA CHANCELLOR

The story of how Laura Chancellor made it to the end of the world's oldest and most prestigious 160km (100-mile) ultramarathon, the Western States 100-Mile Endurance Race.

REBORN ON THE RUN: MY JOURNEY FROM ADDICTION TO ULTRAMARATHONS

CATRA CORBETT

From former meth addict to ultra-running legend, Catra Corbett tells her unlikely story of how she became the first American woman to run more than a hundred 100-mile races.

RUNNING BEYOND: EPIC ULTRA, TRAIL AND SKYRUNNING RACES

IAN CORLESS

Ian Corless explores the rise of ultra-running through interviews with elite athletes, stirring photography and iconic races.

THE RISE OF THE ULTRA-RUNNERS: A JOURNEY TO THE EDGE OF HUMAN ENDURANCE

ADHARANAND FINN

Finn dives into the world of ultra-running to understand why the sport is among the fastest-growing on Earth.

SKY RUNNER: FINDING STRENGTH, HAPPINESS, AND BALANCE IN YOUR RUNNING

EMELIE FORSBERG

Emelie Forsberg shares her passion for sky running through helpful tips, techniques and even recipes.

RUNNER: A SHORT STORY ABOUT A LONG RUN

LIZZY HAWKER

From our *Running Wild*'s Great Himalaya Trail guide, here's an inspiring account of Lizzy Hawker's trail running across the globe, from her first Ultra-Trail du Mont-Blanc to her adventures in the Himalayas.

ABOVE THE CLOUDS: HOW I CARVED MY OWN PATH TO THE TOP OF THE WORLD

KILIAN JORNET

Kilian Jornet chronicles his record-breaking mountain run to the top of Mount Everest.

EAT AND RUN: MY UNLIKELY JOURNEY TO ULTRAMARATHON GREATNESS

SCOTT JUREK

Eat and Run explores the relationship between food and endurance sport through Jurek's own experiences growing up in the Midwest USA, embracing veganism and storming the world of ultra-running.

ULTRAMARATHON MAN: CONFESSIONS OF AN ALL-NIGHT RUNNER

DEAN KARNAZES

The memoir of one of ultra-running's true legends, Dean Karnazes, whose exploits have taken him across the globe, from the South Pole to Death Valley.

BORN TO RUN: THE HIDDEN TRIBE, THE ULTRA-RUNNERS AND THE GREATEST RACE THE WORLD HAS NEVER SEEN

CHRISTOPHER MCDOUGALL

A team of elite ultra-runners learn and run with the Tarahumara, a Mexican Indian tribe who live in the canyons and are some of the best long-distance runners on Earth.

50 RACES TO RUN BEFORE YOU DIE: THE ESSENTIAL GUIDE TO 50 EPIC FOOT-RACES ACROSS THE GLOBE

TOBIAS MEWS

Tobias Mews, who wrote and photographed our *Running Wild* chapter about the Pyrenees, brings together fifty of the world's greatest runs, from Great British peaks to arid deserts.

CONTRIBUTORS

GEORGE BAUER

(WORDS)

Freelance creative, writer, cook and runner.

IG: @__georgebauer
www.airelibre.run/scotland-local

ALEXIS BERG

(PHOTOGRAPHY)

Paris-based outdoor and sports photographer, writer and director. Author of books *Grand Trail* and *The Finishers*, and the film *La Barkley Sans Pitié*.

IG: @alexis_berg
www.alexisberg.com

STEFANIE BISHOP

(WORDS)

USA-based adventuress, ultra-endurance athlete (24+ hour multi-sport) and coach.

IG: @stefadventures
www.stefaniebishop.com

JENNA CRAWFORD

(WORDS)

LA-based runner, community builder and marketer.

IG: @jennavieve_

ANDRÉS FIGUEROA

(PHOTOGRAPHY)

Sports and outdoor videographer and photographer.

IG: @andrewbrndwn

JULIE FREEMAN

(WORDS & PHOTOGRAPHY)

Co-founder and art director of *Like the Wind* magazine, Swiss exile in London.

IG: @sistak

SIMON FREEMAN

(WORDS & PHOTOGRAPHY)

Co-founder and editor of *Like the Wind* magazine. Passionate about inspiring more people to get out on the trails.

IG: @simonbfreeman
www.simonfreeman.co.uk

ANNA GATTA
(WORDS)

Swedish-born, Chamonix-based trail runner and real-estate agent.

DAVIDE GRAZIELLI
(WORDS)

Italy-based runner and co-founder of Destination Unknown running coaching company.

IG: @dgrazielli
www.ducoaching.com

LIZZY HAWKER
(WORDS)

Ultra-runner, five-time UTMB winner, environmental scientist and writer. Moving between Switzerland and Nepal. Author of *Runner* and race director of the Ultra Tour Monte Rosa.

IG: @lizzy.hawker
www.lizzyhawker.com

LINDA HELLAND
(WORDS & PHOTOGRAPHY)

Norwegian travel writer, aiming to inspire others towards active holidays and an active lifestyle in general.

IG: @lindahelland
www.trailspotting.no

DANIEL ALMAZÁN KLINCKWORT & ANA LAFRAMBOISE
(PHOTOGRAPHY)

Dan and Ana – photographers, and husband and wife – live in Mexico and work worldwide. Dan is the co-founder of running experiences organization Aire Libre.

IG: @dklinckwort
@analaframboise
www.airelibre.run

ROB KRAR
(WORDS)

Ultra-running endurance athlete and coach. Organizes running camps for all levels in Arizona with his wife Christina.

IG: @robkrar
www.robkrar.com

EMMA LATHAM PHILLIPS
(WORDS)

Freelance writer with special interests in food and agroecology.

IG: @emmalathamphillips_

IMOGEN LEES
(WORDS)

Like the Wind magazine magazine co-editor, currently based in Norwich, UK.

IG: @looksbetterinsequins

TOM LE LIEVRE
(WORDS)

UK-based trail runner and running coach.

IG: @tom.lelievre

RICKY LIGHTFOOT
(WORDS)

Fells and trail runner based in the Lake District in the UK. Proud dad and firefighter.

IG: @rickylightfoot

JAMES Q. MARTIN
(PHOTOGRAPHY)

Arizona-based *National Geographic* adventure photographer, film-maker and community builder. Directed the film *Rob Krar: Running with Depression*.

IG: @jamesqmartin
www.jamesqmartin.com
www.qstories.com

HILARY MATHESON
(WORDS & PHOTOGRAPHY)

Award-winning Canadian photographer and graphic designer. Ultra-runner.

IG: @thehilaryann
www.thehilaryann.com

TOBIAS MEWS
(WORDS & PHOTOGRAPHY)

Adventure athlete and journalist. Author of *50 Races to Run Before You Die* and *Go!*. Co-Owner of @secretpyrenees and founder of @hardastrails.

IG: @tobiasmews
www.hardastrails.com

BRIAN NEVINS
(PHOTOGRAPHY)

Photographer and film-maker out of New Hampshire, USA.

IG: @nevinsphoto
www.briannevins.com

CHRIS ORD
(PHOTOGRAPHY)

Journalist in adventure media, former editor of *Trail Run Mag Australia* and founder of trail-running adventure company Tour de Trails.

IG: @onewildlife
www.tourdetrails.com

MELISSA & GUY OVERNEY BURNIER
(PHOTOGRAPHY)

Swiss-based travel enthusiasts, food and mountain lovers.

IG: @c_est_meo

GUILLAUME PERETTI
(WORDS)

French ultra-trail runner born and based in Corsica. Lover of mountain biking, road biking and ski mountaineering. Loves sharing his passion of nature with others.

IG: @guillaume_peretti

DAMIEN ROSSO
(PHOTOGRAPHY)

Outdoor and sports photographer based in France.

IG: @drozphoto
www.droz-photo.com

CHRIS SHANE
(PHOTOGRAPHY)

Photographer, film-maker and outdoor athlete based in Maine, USA.

IG: @chrismshane
www.chrismshane.com

REUBEN TABNER
(PHOTOGRAPHY)

Scotland-based travel, action, lifestyle and adventure sports photographer.

IG: @reubentabner
www.reubentabner.co.uk

ALEX TREADWAY
(PHOTOGRAPHY)

Photographer specializing in travel, documentary, sport and adventure. Lives in the UK, works anywhere.

IG: @alextreadway
www.alextreadway.co.uk

ACKNOWLEDGMENTS
JULIE & SIMON FREEMAN

We would like to thank Imogen Lees, our indefatigable deputy editor, who pulled out all the stops to put this book together; designer Fergus McHugh, who was one of our first illustrators for *Like the Wind* magazine; and the team at Thames & Hudson for their trust and support in making *Running Wild*. We are immensely grateful to those who have contributed to the book, but also to the hundreds of contributors to *Like the Wind* magazine who have supported us since 2014 with their words, photography, illustrations and design – in particular Alex Murphy, Laura Funk and David Gardiner. Last, but not least, a massive Thank You to all *Like the Wind* magazine's readers and subscribers for their loyalty.

PICTURE CREDITS

A = Above, B = Below, L = Left, R = Right

Page 1 © Brian Nevins; page 2 © James Q. Martin; page 6 © Hilary Matheson; page 8A © Damien Rosso; page 8B © Chris Shane; page 10 © Hilary Matheson; page 11A © Alexis Berg; page 11B © Damien Rosso; pages 15–29 © Alexis Berg; page 30 © Linda Helland; pages 31–33 © Alexis Berg; page 34A © Linda Helland; page 34B © Alexis Berg; pages 35–38 © Alexis Berg; page 39 © Linda Helland; pages 44–53 © Julie Freeman; pages 59–67 © Reuben Tabner; pages 73–81 © Damien Rosso; pages 86–93 © Tobias Mews; page 99 © Melissa & Guy Overney Burnier; page 100 © Anna & Philippe Gatta; pages 101–08: © Melissa & Guy Overney Burnier; page 109 © Anna & Philippe Gatta; pages 114–23 © Alex Treadway; page 128 © Gérard Benoît; page 130 © André Meier; page 131 © Roland Gerth; page 132 © Vincent Bourrut; page 133 © Julie & Simon Freeman; page 134A © Vincent Bourrut; page 134B © Simon Freeman; page 135 © Julie Freeman; pages 141–49 © Hilary Matheson; pages 155–56 © Brian Nevins; page 157 © Chris Shane; pages 158–59 © Brian Nevins; page 160 © Chris Shane; page 161 © Brian Nevins; page 162A © Brian Nevins; page 162B © Chris Shane; pages 163–64 © Chris Shane; page 165 © Brian Nevins; pages 170–73 © Alexis Berg; page 174 © James Q. Martin; page 175A © James Q. Martin; page 175B © Alexis Berg; pages 176–77 © James Q. Martin; page 178A © Christina Krar; page 178BL&R © Alexis Berg; pages 179–181 © James Q. Martin; pages 186–98 © Daniel Almazán Klinckwort & Ana Laframboise; pages 200–01 © Andrés Figueroa; page 202A © Daniel Almazán Klinckwort & Ana Laframboise; page 202B © Andrés Figueroa; page 203L © Andrés Figueroa; page 203R © Daniel Almazán Klinckwort & Ana Laframboise; pages 204–06 © Daniel Almazán Klinckwort & Ana Laframboise; page 207A © Daniel Almazán Klinckwort & Ana Laframboise; page 207B © Andrés Figueroa; pages 212–21 © Alex Treadway; pages 226–35 © Chris Ord; pages 238–39 © Alex Treadway; page 240 © Damien Rosso

All illustrations by Fergus McHugh

INDEX

Page numbers in bold refer to main entries; those in italics refer to illustrations.

Front cover: The Dolomites at Passo Giau © Alexis Berg
Back cover: Crossing a suspension bridge in Oaxaca © Daniel Almazán Klinckwort & Ana Laframboise at Aire Libre Running

First published in the United Kingdom in 2022 by
Thames & Hudson Ltd, 181A High Holborn, London WC1V 7QX

First published in the United States of America in 2022 by
Thames & Hudson Inc., 500 Fifth Avenue, New York, New York 10110

For the picture credits, please see page 251

Designed by Fergus McHugh
Copyedited by Imogen Lees and Kirsty Seymour-Ure

The trails described in this book can be challenging and it is your responsibility to take all due care in terms of preparation, utilizing the correct equipment, monitoring the weather conditions as well as vigilance on the trails themselves. Thames & Hudson and the authors cannot be held liable for any injury or loss resulting from the information presented in this publication or should you attempt any of the trails.

British Library Cataloguing-in-Publication Data
A catalogue record for this book is available from the British Library

Library of Congress Control Number 2021943187

ISBN 978-0-500-29561-8

Printed and bound in Slovenia by DZS-Grafik d.o.o.